Impossible Choices

Impossible Choices

The Implications of the Cultural References
in the Novels of Manuel Puig

by Pamela Bacarisse

University of Calgary Press
University of Wales Press

University of Calgary Press
2500 University Drive N.W.
Calgary, Alberta, Canada T2N 1N4

University of Wales Press
6 Gwennyth Street
Cardiff CF2 4YD, Wales

Canadian Cataloguing in Publication Data

Bacarisse, Pamela
    Impossible choices

        Includes bibliographical references and index.
        ISBN 1-895176-21-2 (University of Calgary Press)
        ISBN 0-7083-1191-1 (University of Wales Press)

        1. Puig, Manuel—Criticism and interpretation. 2. Culture
in literature. I. Title.

PQ7798.26.U4Z522 1992   863   C92-091762-3

British Library Cataloguing in Publication Data

A catalogue record for this book is available from the British Library.

Cover design by Jon Paine
Printed and bound in Canada by DW Friesen

⊚ This book is printed on acid-free paper.

For Claire and Benjamin . . . again

Contents

Acknowledgments

I SHOULD LIKE TO thank The British Academy for a generous grant toward a research visit to South America in 1987, in the course of which I was able to consult all Manuel Puig's notes and the first drafts of his novels and plays, as well as his unpublished work. On that occasion he was as uncomplainingly co-operative and supportive as ever, and I only wish that he were still with us so that I could reiterate my affectionate gratitude to him. I was lucky to have him as a friend for so long. It would be impossible to repay the hospitality and help that I have received from the Marcondes de Souza family of Rio de Janeiro over the years: thanks to them, to Manuel Puig's mother, doña Male, and to my friend Anna Maria Esnaty de Villela, working in Rio de Janeiro has always seemed like being on holiday. I am equally indebted to Italo Manzi of Paris and my colleague Keith McDuffie of Pittsburgh for their advice and support, and to Sr. Carlos Puig for permission to quote from his brother's works. Finally, special thanks are due to Benjamin and Michael for their exceptional patience.

Novels by Manuel Puig

RH   *La traición de Rita Hayworth*. Buenos Aires: Editorial Jorge Alvarez, 1968.

Bp   *Boquitas pintadas. Folletín*. Buenos Aires: Editorial Sudamericana, 1969.

BAA   *The Buenos Aires Affair*. Mexico City: Joaquín Mortiz, 1973.

Ebma   *El beso de la mujer araña*. Barcelona: Seix Barral, 1976.

Pa   *Pubis angelical*. Barcelona: Seix Barral, 1979.

Me   *Maldición eterna a quien lea estas páginas*. Barcelona: Seix Barral, 1980.

Sac   *Sangre de amor correspondido*. Barcelona: Seix Barral, 1982.

Cnt   *Cae la noche tropical*. Barcelona: Seix Barral, 1988.

Introduction

THE FREQUENT AND OBTRUSIVE references to works of art, artists, films, actors, composers, operas, plays, philosophers, philosophical systems—even to politicians, political events, and ideologies—in the novels of Manuel Puig create a revealing auxiliary network of correlatives, so that it is surprising that so many of them have been neglected by his critics. At the same time, it is significant that the allusions that have been ignored are those made to areas outside the field of mass culture. Whereas the relationship between the world of film and *La traición de Rita Hayworth, The Buenos Aires Affair, El beso de la mujer araña*, and, to a lesser extent, *Pubis angelical*, has been very competently analyzed over the years, and the effects of the inclusion of tango (and other) lyrics and popular radio serials in *Boquitas pintadas* have also been fruitfully investigated, critical selectivity has often resulted in conclusions that may be judged limited, if not actually misleading.[1] Scant attention has been paid to references to high-

1 *La traición de Rita Hayworth* (Buenos Aires: Editorial Jorge Álvarez; Colección Narradores Argentinos, 1968). All references will be to the 1981 reprint of the second, "complete" Spanish edition (Barcelona: Seix Barral; Nueva Narrativa Hispánica, 1976). *The Buenos Aires Affair* (Mexico City: Joaquín Mortiz; Nueva Narrativa Hispánica, 1973). *El beso de la mujer araña* (Barcelona: Seix Barral; Nueva Narrativa Hispánica, 1976). *Pubis angelical* (Barcelona: Seix Barral: Nueva Narrativa Hispánica, 1979). All references to *Boquitas pintadas. Folletín* (Buenos Aires: Editorial Sudamericana, 1969) will be to the 1982 reprint of the Spanish

brow culture (in the form of art) and to manifestations of culture in a more general sense (philosophy, politics, and other ideological theories), the very specificity of which, in addition to their sometimes being found in uncultured contexts, suggests that their inclusion could not have been arbitrary. Indeed, given the careful craftsmanship of Puig's eight novels,[2] which has never received adequate critical recognition, it is my contention that it would be misguided to suppose that anything in his writing is gratuitous. My aim in this study is to draw attention to the author's conscious craftsmanship by focusing on one particular aspect of it, and in doing so to attempt to show how the references to culture signal and underpin Puig's favorite themes, serving as keys both to authorial attitude and to the often mutually incompatible directions that the texts take.

It is not usual for a critic to feel obliged to defend the technique of a novelist who has enjoyed success both in academic circles and in the mass market, but the fact is that none of Puig's novels has been immune to adverse criticism; this has ranged from a total lack of understanding in the late sixties to expressions of disappointment, condemnation, even antagonism, in more recent years. I have attempted to account for the later manifestations of incomprehension elsewhere,[3] pointing out that at least some of them, born of superficial readings of the earlier works, sprang from the prejudiced and shortsighted viewpoint of those who were unable to discern the positive and innovative value of Puig's refusal to observe what Andreas Huyssen has designated "the Great Divide" between mass culture and the canon of high modernism.[4]

Generally speaking, there were two kinds of reaction to *La traición de Rita Hayworth* and *Boquitas pintadas*. Some critics assumed that the popularity that they eventually achieved must be based on reader identification with the simplistically sentimental values of tango lyrics

---

edition (Barcelona: Seix Barral; Nueva Narrativa Hispánica, 1972).

2 In addition to those listed in n. 1: *Maldición eterna a quien lea estas páginas* (Barcelona: Seix Barral; Nueva Narrativa Hispánica, 1980), *Sangre de amor correspondido* (Barcelona: Seix Barral; Nueva Narrativa Hispánica, 1982), and *Cae la noche tropical* (Barcelona: Seix Barral; Biblioteca Breve, 1988).

3 In particular in *The Necessary Dream: A Study of the Novels of Manuel Puig* (Cardiff: U of Wales P; Totowa, NJ: Barnes & Noble, 1988).

4 Andreas Huyssen, *After the Great Divide: Modernism, Mass Culture and Postmodernism* (Bloomington: Indiana UP; London: Macmillan, 1986).

and Hollywood (and other) melodramas, and, clearly, these forms fell outside the boundaries of the current cultural canon. The texts were therefore seen as lacking in profundity, and the apparent accessibility of the values of the characters and of their colloquial speech patterns was judged their only strength.

Ironically, the later books, in which mass culture is far less in evidence, were then criticized because they were not so easy to read. The second reaction placed much emphasis on the spurious nature of the social paradigms found in mass culture, and in both novels the author's attitude was thought to be entirely demythifying and condemnatory. As time went on, several of the critics who had expressed this point of view—those who were, at least, persuaded of the author's seriousness—showed increasing irritation because of his continued recourse to mimetic, grammatically incorrect, popular discourse, at the same time that—in a way—he seemed to espouse humanistic liberal-bourgeois ideals, both of which were considered inappropriate in radical literature. For these critics the validity of the Great Divide was still unchallengeable if mass art perpetuated discredited social patterns.

This is not to say that there were no studies of the first two or three novels that avoided the trap of Manichaeism,[5] and even the hos-

---

5 Some of the worthwhile criticism published before 1979 (the year that *Pubis angelical* came out) includes: Alicia Borinsky, "Castración y lujos," *Revista Iberoamericana* 90 (1975): 29–45, and *Ver/Ser visto (Notas para una analítica poética)* (Barcelona: Antoni Bosch, 1978); Roberto Echavarren, "La superficie de lectura de *The Buenos Aires Affair,*" *Espiral/Revista* 3 (1977): 147–74, and *"El beso de la mujer araña* y las metáforas del sujeto," *Revista Iberoamericana* 102–03 (1978): 65–75; Iris Josefina Ludmer, *"Boquitas pintadas:* siete recorridos," *Actual* 2.8–9 (1971): 3–22; Alfred J. MacAdam's chapter on Puig in his *Modern Latin American Narratives: The Dreams of Reason* (Chicago: U of Chicago P, 1977): 91–101; Marta Morello-Frosch, *"La traición de Rita Hayworth,* o el nuevo arte de narrar películas," *Sin Nombre* 4.1 (1970): 77–82, and "La sexualidad opresiva en las obras de Manuel Puig," *Nueva Narrativa Hispanoamericana* 5 (1975): 151–58; Ricardo Piglia, "Clase media: cuerpo y destino (una lectura de *La traición de Rita Hayworth* de Manuel Puig)," *Nueva Novela Latinoamericana,* ed. J. Lafforgue, 2 vols. (Buenos Aires: Editorial Paidós, 1972) 2: 350–62; Emir Rodríguez Monegal, *"La traición de Rita Hayworth:* una tarea de desmitificación," and "Los sueños de Evita: a propósito de la última novela de Manuel Puig," both in *Narradores de esta América,* ed. Emir Rodríguez Monegal (Buenos Aires: Editorial Alfa Argentina, 1974) 2: 356–80, 381–93; Margery A. Safir, "Mitología: otro nivel de metalenguaje en *Boquitas pintadas,*" *Revista Iberoamericana* 90 (1975): 47–58; Severo Sarduy, "Notas a las notas a las notas . . . a propósito de Manuel Puig," *Revista Iberoamericana*

tility toward the later works, particularly *Maldición eterna a quien lea estas páginas* (1980) and *Sangre de amor correspondido* (1982), has been counterbalanced by some impressively clearsighted analysis.[6] Though this has come too late for the author himself,[7] it is gratifying to note that at the present time some journalists and many academic commentators are beginning to take the entire corpus of his writings very seriously indeed, the latter classifying him as one of Latin America's first postmodern authors and by far the most impressive representative of the Latin American Post-Boom. Indeed, there is little to complain about in current Puig criticism; nevertheless, to the best of my knowledge, the homogeneity of attitudes and techniques that lies behind variations in novelistic format has still not been examined thoroughly, and contemporary re-evaluation of the books in the context of postmodern writing, postmodern culture, and current sociopolitical ideology, albeit appropriate and long overdue, may run the risk of reasserting the false hegemony of popular culture throughout the texts.

Nevertheless, given my aim of highlighting the author's even-handedness regarding his auxiliary allusions, it would be counterproductive to ignore completely the references to the so-called *géneros menores* [minor genres] that were so dear to him, even though so much has already been written on the topic.[8] Indeed, Puig's affection for

---

37 (1971): 555–67; and Gilberto Triviños, "La destrucción del verosímil folletinesco en *Boquitas pintadas,*" *Texto Crítico* 9 (1976): 117–30.

6 For example: Sharon Magnarelli, "Manuel Puig's *Betrayed by Rita Hayworth*: Betrayed by the Cross-Stitch," chapter 6 in her *The Lost Rib: Female Characters in the Spanish-American Novel* (Lewisburg, PA: Bucknell UP, 1985); René Alberto Campos, *Espejos: la textura cinemática en* La traición de Rita Hayworth (Madrid: Editorial Pliegos, 1985) 117–46; Lucille Kerr, *Suspended Fictions: Reading Novels by Manuel Puig* (Urbana: U of Illinois P, 1987); Roberto Echavarren and Enrique Giordano, *Manuel Puig: montaje y alteridad del sujeto* (Santiago, Chile: Instituto Profesional del Pacífico, 1986), though this, in fact, contains the Echavarren articles already referred to (see above, n. 5); and Philip Swanson, "Sailing Away on a Boat to Nowhere: *El beso de la mujer araña* and *Kiss of the Spider Woman,* from Novel to Film," *Essays on Hispanic Themes in Honour of Edward C. Riley,* eds. Jennifer Lowe and Philip Swanson (Edinburgh: Dept. of Hispanic Studies, University of Edinburgh, 1989).

7 Manuel Puig died unexpectedly, at the age of fifty-seven, in 1990.

8 See Saúl Sosnowski, "Manuel Puig: Entrevista," *Hispamérica* 3 (1973): 73, and Emir Rodríguez Monegal, "El folletín rescatado," *Revista de la Universidad de México* 27.2 (1972): 27–35.

popular culture—for which, even if he had not discussed it in interviews, supporting evidence can easily be found through close readings of the texts—is the key to one of my principal conclusions: that one of the most strikingly postmodern features of his writing is ambivalence.

I shall therefore be considering examples of both "high" and "low" culture, which constitute an intertext, though I am using this term somewhat loosely.[9] What is of interest here is specific quotation, and this demands the investigation of indicated models, rather than reflecting Julia Kristeva's well-known theory of intertextuality, inspired by Bakhtin, which posits the interdependence of any text with *all* its transposed (and suppressed) predecessors. The relation between Puig's texts and the cultural elements referred to in them (though these may not necessarily be literary) can, I think, be categorized as intertextual; the references help the reader to discern more clearly the nature of the preoccupations of the main texts, which are thus communicated without determination. Because they are quoted and not suppressed, they fall into the *intentional* category signalled by Todorov in his reading of Bakhtin;[10] their inclusion is a conscious authorial device, the existence of which is one of the factors that give rise to my espousal of the Formalists' view of the writer as craftsman.

Although this critical position is unusual when dealing with a postmodern author, it is authorial *Weltanschauung*, the view of the function and nature of literature, and the provenance of source materials that are subject to changing sociocultural forces, rather than modes of creation and production. Even as theorizing goes in different directions, a certain consistency can occasionally be detected: the Formalists' stance is not all that far removed from later judgments, such as that of Roland Barthes, who (in *S/Z*) concentrated on the pro-

---

9 In fact, there is little consensus of opinion as to what actually constitutes an intertext. It can be "a text (or set of texts) that is cited, rewritten, prolonged, or generally transformed by another text and that makes the latter meaningful," or, according to Laurent Jenny, it can be the *principal* text, which "absorbs and binds together a multiplicity of other texts." Finally, in the view of Michel Arrivé, it is "a set of texts that are intertextually linked." See Gerald Prince, *A Dictionary of Narratology* (Lincoln: U of Nebraska P, 1987).

10 Tzvetan Todorov, *Mikhail Bakhtin: The Dialogical Principle*, trans. Wlad Godzich (Manchester: Manchester UP; *Theory and History of Literature*, vol. 13, 1984): 74.

duction of the text, or even that of the Marxist critic Pierre Macherey, for whom the writer is a producer.[11]

The specificity of Puig's allusions to culture signals their function as an invitation to the reader to participate actively in the production of a *scriptible* text. In theory, and (presumably) in intention, all of them are equally suggestive, but in practice, the initial impact of the author's utilization and appreciation of mass culture has tended to distort critical reception, and it is this unbalanced view that has changed little over the years.[12] Were it not so, it might be supposed that, in the first place, the reaction of the reader would have been a certain sense of disorientation, perhaps accompanied by a feeling of alienation—in some cases because of the contextual incongruity of the citation, in others because of the seemingly excessive quantity of names and titles furnished, but always because the narrative has been unduly interrupted and disturbed. Then, he or she should perhaps have been intrigued by the challenge being issued by the novelist. Some examples are: in *El beso de la mujer araña*, at the moment when Molina, whose intellect, education, and background have previously been unfavorably contrasted with those of his bourgeois cellmate, suddenly and incongruously mentions Sparafucile, a character from Verdi's opera *Rigoletto*; in *Pubis angelical*, when Ana provides so many unnecessary details of performances at the Teatro Colón—and elsewhere—in Buenos Aires; and when, for a reason that is not immediately apparent, the brutish and philistine Héctor (in *La traición de Rita Hayworth*) reveals the names of the authors that he refuses to read. There are many more examples: in *La traición de Rita Hayworth*, the reader is told the titles of Mita's two favorite novels; Gladys, in *The Buenos Aires Affair*, is unaccountably reluctant to attend a Rouault exhibition (she sees Leo, the man she loves, in terms of Matisse paintings); in the same text, each chapter is

---

11 See David Forgacs, "Marxist Literary Theories," in *Modern Literary Theory: A Comparative Introduction*, eds. Ann Jefferson and David Robey, 2nd ed. (London: B.T. Batsford, 1986) 166–203 (177).

12 When Manuel Puig died, many obituaries placed untoward emphasis on his fascination with Hollywood, even though this had become less and less evident in his work. The headline of one of them read, "The Novelist as Moviegoer," (*The Guardian*, 24 July 1990), while the writer of another classified him as "Latin America's movie-man made novelist," and then—almost automatically, it seems—went on to call him "a literary lightweight." (Andrew Graham-Youll, "Manuel Puig," *The Independent*, 24 July 1990).

prefaced by a still and dialogue from an old film; three of the vital lost texts in *Maldición eterna a quien lea estas páginas* are identified, and the connection between them is by no means obvious. Now that we are accustomed to the juxtaposition of all kinds of models in literature, the device as such would almost certainly stimulate curiosity regarding authorial purpose, but in the sixties and early seventies it proved impossible to avoid concentrating on the elements taken from mass culture. (It is significant that, from the above list, only the relationship between the epigraphs and the text of *The Buenos Aires Affair* has been analyzed.)

Whatever the period, no reader can be compelled to accept implicit invitations to take part in the creation of a text—not completing it, but at least making it more comprehensive; in any case, as I have already pointed out in a published article, the technique is not without its pitfalls.[13] In the first place, because of their eclectic nature, reader recognition of the implications of all the references is virtually impossible: apparently the author is hoping for (if not taking for granted) an unrealistic breadth of extratextual knowledge. Furthermore, even when the implications of some of the allusions are recognized, the occasional incongruity could prove irritating, as could the constant interruptions of the flow of the narrative—the lengthy footnotes in *El beso de la mujer araña* are a case in point.[14] Finally, the inclusion of contemporary, sometimes even local, cultural elements will almost certainly underline the ephemerality of the principal text, diminishing the possibility of its being included in the modernist canon, which demands totalizing universality.

However, although no one could respond to all the references, some of these will be recognized by many readers, and it is the purpose of this study to draw attention to the others. As for incongruity, we find that this is not unacceptably frequent, and that when it is

---

13 Pamela Bacarisse, "Manuel Puig and the Uses of Culture," *The Review of Contemporary Fiction* 2.3 (1991): 197–207.

14 According to Yves Macchi, "le texte B [the footnotes], qui n'est qu'un long résumé didactique et complexe de diverses théories psychanalytiques, a pour effet d'éloigner le lecteur du fil du dialogue ou des narrations de Molina" [the effect of text B, which is just a long didactic and complex summary of different psychoanalytic theories, is to distance the reader from the main thread of the dialogue or Molina's stories]. "Fonction narrative des notes infrapaginales dans *El beso de la mujer araña* de Manuel Puig," *Les Langues Néo-Latines* 76 (1982): 67–81 (69–70).

discernible the author is quite deliberately signalling the incompatibility that exists between a character's milieu and cultural influences. For example, whereas there is relatively little interest in High Art among the majority of the *dramatis personae* of *Boquitas pintadas* and *Sangre de amor correspondido* (both set among uneducated people who live in isolated, philistine surroundings), there is a surprising number of highbrow allusions in *La traición de Rita Hayworth*, which has the same bleak setting as *Boquitas pintadas*. There is an obvious, though superficial, explanation for their presence in *La traición de Rita Hayworth*, where many of the characters are children in the process of being educated who are forced into contact with a world that the majority of the adults have never known or have long since forgotten. Even so, the incongruous references reveal that many of the characters in this novel have different standards, aims, and horizons from those of their neighbors.

The characters in *La traición de Rita Hayworth* can fruitfully be compared with the protagonists of *Boquitas pintadas*. Although Coronel Vallejos is so small, not one of the characters from the first book (*RH*) reappears, even peripherally, in the second (*Bp*), and Puig once admitted that this was entirely deliberate. *La traición de Rita Hayworth* is an elaborated autobiography—"Toto soy yo" [I am Toto], he once said—and it concentrates on those who, like himself, were different: prey to nervous tension, alienated, frustrated, and disillusioned.[15] They look for consolation outside their immediate environment and its cultural icons. *Boquitas pintadas*, on the other hand, was inspired by a visit the author made to his hometown of General Villegas (the Coronel Vallejos of the two novels) after an absence of eleven years; on this occasion he was struck by the air of sadness that characterized the rest of the community, those who had tried to conform and to

---

15 Puig talked about the genesis of this novel in an interview with Jean-Michel Fossey, published in *Galaxia Latinoamericana* (Las Palmas: Inventarios Provisionales, 1973) 137–52. Part of it had already appeared in the Uruguayan journal *Marcha* (14 July 1972). What he never revealed publicly was that as a child his nickname was Coco. In the opening conversation of the first draft of *La traición*, originally entitled *Pájaros en la cabeza*, in which he had not yet changed the names of the real-life source characters, his aunt refers to the baby she is longing to see for the first time as "el Coco."

observe the rules of the game that society had demanded they play.[16] The escape routes that their more aware contemporaries seemed to have discovered with their adhesion to the values found in highbrow works of art, often with exotic origins, had not been open to them. In the end, unrealistic paradigms betray both groups.

Ironically, since their horizons are so much broader, the characters in *La traición de Rita Hayworth* are even more disillusioned than their counterparts in *Boquitas pintadas*, those who were influenced only by mass culture. It is reasonable to infer from this situation that, from the point of view of human emancipation from unnecessary suffering and social injustice, there is a negative aspect to the question of parity in cultural values: at times, Puig seems to suggest that there is little to choose between mass culture and High Art, not because they are equally valuable but because they are equally and perniciously misleading.

Molina, in *El beso de la mujer araña*, is an amalgam of the two microcosms. Like Nené and her friends in *Boquitas pintadas*, he is a slave to the mass media—in his case the cinema and the lyrics of boleros—but he is also unaccountably knowledgeable about other areas of culture, particularly opera.[17] Whatever else his personality and tastes connote, the character of Molina once again underlines the fact that for Puig there was no vital difference between highbrow and lowbrow art, which are both valid indicators of personal and collective truths; furthermore, it is quite possible to be attracted to, and betrayed by, both. The originality of this approach lies in the fact that the texts focus on a subjective aesthetic, not the arbitrarily imposed standards of the day. Puig's admission that he found much popular art very beautiful was undeniably sincere, but it tended to confirm the view that this was all that interested him.[18] In fact, he was also widely read and knowledgeable about High Art, and although he was at pains to conceal this, it is visible, if not obvious, in his writing.

As for the limiting nature of the cultural allusions, it would appear that everything depends on the equilibrium obtained between them

---

16 See M. Osorio, "Entrevista con Manuel Puig," *Cuadernos para el diálogo* 231 (1977): 51–53.

17 Puig himself was a great lover of nineteenth-century opera. It may be relevant that one side of his family originated in the Italian town of Busseto, where Giuseppe Verdi was brought up.

18 Rodríguez Monegal, "El folletín," 32.

and the main text. Manuel Puig was by no means the first author to include factual references in his fiction, and there are countless well-known texts in existence where it may be judged essential to recognize and understand these, and for which in later epochs—or in other countries—explanatory footnotes are deemed necessary.[19] It may well be a question of quantity. If there are too many, the narrative line is obscured. The fact that Puig's books have achieved so much success even though one section of the cultural references has been neglected tends to suggest that in his case they have not had a negative impact.

Indeed, in the same way that the footnotes to *El beso de la mujer araña* are a vital ingredient of the work as a whole, so the cultural allusions add an extra dimension to the interpretation of all the texts. There is little doubt in my mind that Puig felt that any risk that their inclusion might involve was worth taking. I suggest that, ultimately, they establish an intertextual relation in which it is less a question of a privileged text drawing on a background system of signification than a process in which apparently auxiliary textual elements, in the form of indicated texts (or other codes), can become almost homologous with the narrative, with the explicit and the implied texts cross-referring to each other by means of the reader's contribution. Then suspected patterns may be confirmed, and in some instances new interpretative avenues present themselves. One example is the point in *Pubis angelical* when Ana dreams of a world as beautiful as a duet from Mozart's *Così fan tutte*.

It is, first of all, Puig's cultural egalitarianism that I hope to demonstrate, treating equally the references that are made explicitly and those that are made unknowingly. Even if, in other cases, it is essential to distinguish between the concept of authorial intention and what Seymour Chatman has recently designated textual "intent,"[20] in this context it is impossible to deny that the former is an appropriate area of investigation.

---

19 There are thousands of examples, but one that immediately springs to mind is *La Voluntad* (1902), by the Spanish '98 Generation writer José Martínez Ruiz ("Azorín"): here the characters' views on contemporary Spanish society, and on humanity in general, which constitute the novel's principal interest, are linked to real-life personalities, movements, and events, most of which have now been forgotten, even in Spain.

20 Seymour Chatman, *Coming to Terms: The Rhetoric of Narrative in Fiction and Film* (Ithaca: Cornell UP, 1990) 74 *et seq.*

At the same time, I shall draw attention to a postmodern lack of certainty—indeed, to constant ambivalence—which is encapsulated in repeated authorial emphasis on the question of ineluctable but impossible choices: choices that human beings are obliged to make between two equally pernicious options. Paradoxically, there is no lack of determinism in Puig, and there is also evidence of the fundamental pessimism that must inevitably accompany any deterministic viewpoint.[21] Nevertheless, nothing can be definitely determined in his work. Perhaps ambivalence itself is life-affirming, as Eugene Goodheart has said, claiming that it suggests "not incapacity, but power. It encompasses contradictoriness and conflict. As a mode of contradiction, ambivalence represents an opening to experience, it includes rather than excludes."[22] In many cases it "assumes a binarism, each term of which offers a dismal prospect,"[23] and though this may indeed be an accurate vision of the world and of Manuel Puig's own view of it, the ambivalence that can be located in his writings does denote the power of human resilience, based on desire and manifested in a fundamental, though ill-fated, rejection of both alternatives.

Two problems presented themselves in the preparation of this study. The first concerned the criteria that should dictate a process of selection from the vast number of references; the second, how to organize their presentation so as to eliminate repetition and ensure that patterns emerged. When choosing the references, I tried to avoid rehearsing what has already been published on mass culture, but I have indicated in the notes where the most helpful studies can be located. The question of the disposition of the material was more taxing. A tentative division into genres (film, opera, novels, poetry, etc.) resulted in duplication; dealing with each character or novel separately obscured thematic unity; creating a dictionary of allusions gave rise to overlapping, with the added disadvantage of providing insufficient space for comment. Ultimately, I decided to start from a general concept and to illustrate this with particular examples. The chosen references will therefore be found in sections devoted to a theme, sub-theme, situation, or attitude, and I have added a separate

---

21 For more on this, see my article, "Manuel Puig's *sentimiento trágico de la vida*," *World Literature Today* 65.4 (1991): 631–36, in which I compare his outlook with that of Miguel de Unamuno.

22 Eugene Goodheart, *Desire and its Discontents* (New York: Columbia UP, 1991) 52.

23 Goodheart, *Desire*, 52.

index of those artists, authors, works, and fictional characters that come under discussion in the main body of the text, together with the disciplines they suggest, such as psychoanalysis, astrology, feminism, and religion.

I

Sexuality

THE SUPERIOR MAN

IT COMES AS NO surprise that in the pre-feminist world investigated by Manuel Puig the concept of the irresistible "hombre superior" [superior man]—wise, intelligent, and with an inborn right to power—should preoccupy so many of his characters. One of these is Ana, the protagonist of *Pubis angelical*, who is so convinced of its mythic dimension that, at least initially, she is unperturbed by her inability to define or defend it (*Pa* 19). On the other hand, her Mexican friend Beatriz sees Ana's unrealistic desires as no more than the result of patriarchal conditioning.[1] Her exasperation appears to be entirely justified, especially since she points out that any woman who judges herself inferior would be foolish to yearn for someone who would constantly confirm this. As she says, such a relationship could not possi-

---

1 The heroine of Puig's short story "Aborde del Concord" (sic) [Aboard the Concorde], which appeared in the now-defunct Spanish journal *Bazaar*, also claims that women are inhibited "por culpa de siglos de represión" [because of centuries of repression]. On the other hand, in *Cae la noche tropical* one of the two female protagonists (who, admittedly, are over eighty) wonders if this is so: "Ahora la moda es decir que las mujeres habríamos nacido así también, baguales como ellos [los hombres], pero que la educación nos cambió. Pero para saber a ciencia cierta si eso es verdad habría que nacer de nuevo" [It's fashionable now to say that we women are born that way too, as wild as men are, but that our upbringing changes us. But to be absolutely sure whether that's true or not, you'd have to be born again] (97).

bly lead to self-improvement on the part of the woman: "Si un hombre se acerca a una mujer de algún modo inferior, es porque le gusta así como es" [If a man takes an interest in a woman who is inferior in some way, it's because he likes her as she is] (*Pa* 20).[2]

Indeed, Beatriz would seem to be the ideal role model for Ana, who is aware of feminism but cannot bring herself to espouse it, even though her adherence to patriarchal values has not made her happy and her longstanding attitude may be judged as self-defeating as Molina's exaggerated "femininity" in *El beso de la mujer araña*. Though a busy, educated woman with a mind of her own and a strong ethical sense, Beatriz is nevertheless a contented wife and mother; she is also unusually sympathetic toward her own sex. It is tempting to join her in condemning Ana out of hand, but it is my contention that to do this would be to ignore the dilemma that exercises the author, who never furnishes clearcut solutions to life's problems and who is always primarily concerned with the question of human happiness.[3]

Although Beatriz has indeed found fulfilment, she is an unrealistically fortunate member of a new generation of women that has dared to challenge a society riddled with *machismo*, one in which "males have produced language, thought and reality."[4] She is, in fact, the emblem-

---

2 That this problem interested the author greatly is confirmed by its presence in some of his early writings. For example, the heroine of his unpublished filmscript *La tajada* [The Cut] (1960), who comes from a vulgar and pretentious background, is swept off her feet by a sophisticated older man, then seduced by a rich young man from an important family (here, as in the case of Valentín in *El beso de la mujer araña*, Puig uses the term "de apellido" [from a good family]). She hopes to learn from them and improve herself, but they are determined that she stay as she is.

3 Puig himself was very conscious of his own ambivalence, and claimed that it was not typical in an Argentine. In an unpublished piece that was to be called either "Chistes sobre argentinos" [Jokes about Argentines] or "El último tango en Venezuela" [Last Tango in Venezuela], he maintained that in Argentina "hay que proyectar convencimiento en las ideas que se plantean" [you have to project an air of conviction regarding any idea you propose], whereas he was uncharacteristically content merely to understand an opposing viewpoint: "El simple hecho de comprender su error ya me satisface y a otra cosa" [Just understanding where they've gone wrong is enough, and I get on with something else].

4 Dale Spender, *Man Made Language*, 2nd ed. (London: Routledge & Kegan Paul, 1985) 143.

atically ideal example of fusion between what is best in the traditional female role and what is desirable for the New Woman. Nevertheless, Ana suspects that there is much to be lost in emulating her, for she recalls not only the excitement of anticipation as she waited for a superior man to appear, but also her happiness, albeit shortlived, when he actually did.[5] Puig may well be juxtaposing two manifestations of utopianism in his portrayal of these women.[6]

Eventually, Ana is obliged to make a definitive choice, and she opts for "wisdom" rather than "pleasure," relinquishing her quest for a superior man.[7] The incautious reader may see this as constituting a truly happy ending, and it may be significant that, were this the case, it would be a level of determination unique in Puig's writings. In fact, given her upbringing, any possibility of her again enjoying the kind of happiness that she once knew has now been eliminated; as the author himself once pointed out, it is far from easy for people to change their views about sexuality and gender roles, and if a woman like Ana does so, her capacity for "wonderful adventures of the imagination" will be

---

5 Puig constantly emphasizes the ephemeral and illusory nature of happiness. For example, *El beso de la mujer araña* ends: "Este sueño es corto pero es feliz" [This dream is short, but it is happy] (287). In an unpublished (and, as far as I know, untitled) play, the author has one of his female creations rejoice, *post mortem*, that she died before her lover's desire could wane: "He muerto yo antes que tu deseo" [I have died before your desire could], and she considers this a "final feliz" [happy ending] to their story: "Acabo siendo un espectro, pero un espectro amado" [I am now a ghost, but one that is loved].

6 The situation of Silvia in *Cae la noche tropical* is not entirely dissimilar, even though she does not eschew the dictates of the heart. After a brush with death, "prometió que nunca más le iba a dar importancia a pavadas, y que iba a gozar de la vida" [she promised that she would never again attach importance to stupid things, and that she was going to enjoy life] (51). In the event, life does not turn out to be as enjoyable as she had hoped, and she even attempts suicide.

7 These are George Yúdice's terms for the two alternatives: "*El beso de la mujer araña y Pubis angelical*: entre el placer y el saber," *Literature and Popular Culture*, ed. Rose S. Minc (Gaithersburg: Ediciones Hispamérica and Montclair State College, 1981) 43–57. See also Karen S. Christian, "El mito del 'hombre superior' y la liberación de la mujer colonizada en *Pubis angelical*," *Alba de América* 4.6–7 (1986): 93–103, and my "Superior Men and Inferior Reality: Manuel Puig's *Pubis angelical*," *Bulletin of Hispanic Studies* 66.1 (1989): 361–70.

lost.[8] Moreover, in spite of his oft-professed horror of *machismo*, Puig was only too aware that, as its hold weakened in certain areas, new problems had arisen. These include the apparent impossibility of establishing a workable relationship between the sexes.[9] Silvia, in his last novel, *Cae la noche tropical*, is singularly unsuccessful when she decides to take the initiative in a relationship, and is judged—explicitly by one of the elderly protagonists, and implicitly by the reluctant lover—"una cargosa" [a nuisance] (135).

In spite of the indications to the contrary which have been noted by some critics, all Puig's novels reveal his reservations on the subject of liberation if this involves disregarding the imagination. Clearly, the fact that in the past this has been programmed by the patriarchy has resulted in inequality and injustice, but even unrealistic, illusory, and wrongheaded dreams are portrayed as consolatory, life-enhancing predicates to human desire.

Until recently, most fiction, together with other representational aspects of culture, has reflected and approvingly celebrated the traditional values found in dreams whose morphology has been constructed and imposed by the powerful, thereby perpetuating the status quo: norms relating to superiority and inferiority have been systematized, and received opinions have continually been reinforced. In the context of male-female relations, the historical result needs no elaboration: literature (or opera, or the fine arts, or film) did not invent male power, but has always served to confirm its unassailable nature. Ironically, though male arrogance, ruthlessness, treachery, and cruelty are so frequently depicted in them, these works have brought pleasure to female audiences (represented by Puig's female creations, among whom Molina and Toto should be included), as well as to those men who are accidentally or constitutionally incapable of meeting the

---

8 In J.-Michel Quiblier and J.-Pierre Joecker, "Entretien avec Manuel Puig," *Masques: Revue des homosexualités* 11 (1981): 29–32, Puig observes that, unfortunately, there is an age "où tout se cristallise, l'érotisme en particulier. Il est par la suite très difficile d'oublier certains rôles pour en adopter de nouveaux" [when everything sets hard, particularly in the erotic field. It is therefore very difficult to relinquish certain roles and adopt new ones] (31). This was also the occasion on which he referred to the loss of "une grande aventure de l'imagination" [wonderful adventures of the imagination] (32).

9 Elisabeth Pérez Luna, "Con Manuel Puig en Nueva York," *Hombre del mundo* 8 (1978): 69–107.

demands of stereotyped roles. It is this anomaly that many of Puig's cultural allusions illustrate.

In some cases, these cultural references help to account for the narrative presence of (what appears to be) inexplicable female collusion with the dictates of a system that is unsympathetic toward women. In *La traición de Rita Hayworth*, for example, Mita—who is far from happily married to a boorish, egocentric, and unstable man—reveals touching sympathy for the heroine of the film *Hasta que la muerte nos separe* (RH 141, 143), the popularity of which reflected universal acceptance of woman's traditional role of self-effacing and suffering helpmeet.[10] In English it was called *The Great Man's Lady* (with Barbara Stanwyck and Joel McCrea, dir. William A. Wellman, 1942), and when both titles are taken into account, it is easy to detect the principle that love, dignity, and security more than compensate for female subservience—a position that, in any case, is justified by the perceived superiority of the man. This is never in doubt, and powerful men are frequently, but unobtrusively, alluded to throughout all the texts; they range from George Washington to the subjects of the Emil Ludwig biographies—Goethe, Napoleon, and Hindenburg—so beloved of Mita (RH 147).[11] The paradigm is also valid for Herminia, who identifies with Mary Todd Lincoln, helpmeet to a another great man (RH 267).

Superiority is often represented by trusted and powerful father images. It is surely no coincidence that in *Boquitas pintadas* Nené and her new husband (whose dullness is far removed from what might be expected of a great man) spend an evening in the theatre seeing *La estancia de papá* [Daddy's Estate], and the fact that this seemingly redundant piece of information is juxtaposed with the revelation that they also attend a puppet show (Bp 150) may indicate the subjugation of both sexes to suspect imposed values. There is also a hint of paternal feet of clay in *La traición de Rita Hayworth*, when Herminia, a frustrated and impecunious spinster, recalls that her late father once assured her that Schubert's life of poverty had a sublime significance (RH 272). She

---

10 There is an explicit parallel in that both Mita and the character played by Barbara Stanwyck in the film lose a baby.

11 Emil Ludwig (1881–1948) produced several of these elaborated biographies, which were actually historical romances. *Goethe* dates from 1920 and *Napoleon* from 1925, but I can find no trace of a life of Hindenburg. The author was almost certainly thinking of *Bismarck* (1926).

has always accepted this dubious assertion, convinced that her father could never have misled her and consoled by its presumed vindication of her squalid lifestyle. This cannot improve until she is willing to challenge the false image of paternal infallibility that lies behind her longing for a husband who would be a surrogate father.

Both the narratives and the cultural references draw the reader's attention to the image of control. The *Ama/Actriz* [Housewife/Actress] in *Pubis angelical*, who is one of Ana's self-projections, is one of its most notable victims.[12] Her story is based on the life of the Austrian film-star Hedy Lamarr, whose first husband kept her locked up and destroyed all the copies of her work prior to their marriage, but who became the prisoner of the film industry when she left him.[13] As Ana faces up to her own impossible choice, the two projected scenarios of the *Ama* and the *Actriz* illustrate her reservations about her options. In them (as well as in the story of W218), she rehearses the arguments against both subservience *and* emancipation.[14] On the one hand, she realizes that male validation will almost certainly provide protection and security, but, as the *Ama* contemplates a beautiful amber liquid, which would be formless unless imprisoned in heavy glass (*Pa* 14–15),[15] she equates the acquisition of identity with its restriction.[16] Being owned, controlled, and incarcerated are thus seen as necessary to the process of becoming a woman.

---

12 See chapter 6, "Only Make-Believe," in my book *The Necessary Dream* for more on the relationship between the three protagonists of this novel.

13 Hedy Lamarr, *Ecstasy and Me: My Life as a Woman* (London: W.H. Allen, 1967) 19, 23. Like the *Ama/Actriz*, Hedy Lamarr was often referred to as "the most beautiful woman in the world."

14 In the *Actriz* projection, she refers to her last, adored lover as "Él" [he], and this has evident messianic overtones.

15 The immediate source of this image may be the well-known *estribillo* to a poem by Amado Nervo (1870–1919), one of Clara Evelia's idols in *The Buenos Aires Affair*: "El agua toma siempre la forma de los vasos / que la contienen" [Water always takes the form of the glasses / that contain it]. "La hermana agua," *Poemas* (1901).

16 It goes without saying that modern feminist thought challenges this assumption. See, for example, Maria Laplace's impressive discussion of the film *Now, Voyager* (1942), in which the heroine's appearance, and life, are transformed by love. "Producing and Consuming the Woman's Film," *Home is Where the Heart Is: Studies in Melodrama and the Woman's Film*, ed. Christine Gledhill (London: British Film Institute, 1987) 138–66 (152).

The relationship between the night-club singer and her rich protector in the (invented) Mexican film in *El beso de la mujer araña* also illustrates this belief (*Ebma* 226 et seq.). Of course, in both these cases, as well as in that of Herminia, it is impossible to avoid the question of female economic dependency, but financial inequality is only one of the reasons for the existence of a power imbalance, by means of which, as Sharon Magnarelli has so rightly observed, "women have always been personae, characters, literary creations, both inside and outside of fiction, continually fantasised, fabricated, and counterfeited."[17] The fact that Ana in *Pubis angelical* and Silvia in *Cae la noche tropical* are not dependent on anyone brings them little comfort; the only thing that does is their faith in rediscovering the joys of caring submissiveness.

Not infrequently, male control involves callous deceitfulness and betrayal. Again, the complaisant reaction of female audiences reveals their faith in the existence of transcendental compensations, as they emulate the forgiving patience and virtue of victimized heroines at the same time as they fall prey to the appeal of *donjuanismo*—the myth of man as sexual hero. It is not without interest that the first piece of music to be placed at the *romería* in *Boquitas pintadas*—a prelude to La Raba's downfall—should be *Don Juan* (believed to be the first tango-song[18]). The title of the novel itself is taken from an Alfredo LePera/ Carlos Gardel foxtrot, *Rubias de Nueva York* [New York Blondes], in which male desire is directed toward all women, rather than one in particular. The lyric is entirely calculating: the *rubias* are "deliciosas criaturas perfumadas" [delectable, scented creatures], with "cabecitas adornadas / que mienten amor" [sweet little dressed-up heads / that pretend to be in love], and it begins with a list of interchangeable girls' names. Although this is no more than a lighthearted celebration of glamorous and exotic showgirls whose "lies" are merely theatrical representation, its selection as the introduction to the indiscriminate promiscuity of the novel's hero and of his friend Pancho, who seduces

---

17 Magnarelli, *The Lost Rib*, 15.

18 Lyric by Ricardo Podestá, music by Ernesto Ponzio, published at the end of the last century. See Raúl González Tuñón, *A la sombra de los barrios amados* (Buenos Aires: Editorial Lautaro, 1957). For an analysis of the *donjuanismo* of the protagonist, Juan Carlos, see Lucille Kerr, *Suspended Fictions* (chapter 3: "A Succession of Popular Designs").

and abandons La Raba, is as significant as the reactions of the women
that they deceive.[19]

In many of the novels, the betrayal of devoted women is indirectly
signalled by means of the mention of (usually well-known) works of
art. These are often nineteenth-century operas, whose values are still
accepted by the majority of Puig's characters; even when the situation
in the second fiction is the result of a genuine misunderstanding, it is
usually exacerbated by pernicious patriarchal attitudes, but the portrayal of female virtue has compensatory mythopoeic power. (It is, perhaps, worth pointing out that while the continued popularity of this
kind of opera is incontrovertibly based on the appeal of the music, it
would be a mistake to see this as the reason for Puig's inclusion of
operatic titles.) For example, Verdi's *Il Trovatore*, (1855), which
Herminia and Toto listen to on the radio (*RH* 277–78), glorifies female
subjugation: in it, the blameless Leonora, who eventually kills herself
rather than denounce the man she loves, is spurned by him when he
suspects her of infidelity. In fact, he too is a victim of what Claude Le
Bigot has designated a pernicious triangle[20] (in other words, he has
his own impossible choice to make), but even so, his attitude reveals
a level of self-righteous confidence that is echoed—on a much less
melodramatic scale—when Berto, Toto's father, removes the radio
before the broadcast has ended.

It is also relevant that Donizetti's *Lucia di Lammermoor* (1835),
which is being performed in the Teatro Colón when Ana meets the
ruthless right-wing Peronist, Alejandro (*Pa* 95), has an innocent heroine
who goes to an early grave because of the prejudices of her lover and
the duplicity of her kinsmen. In this case, a complaisant audience,
which includes Ana, finds comfort in the fact that the hero ultimately—and unnecessarily—forgives her before committing suicide. Later
in the narrative, this plot is reflected in Ana's futuristic fantasy: as her
remorseful and tearful lover, LKJS, saves her (as W218) from a fate
worse than death, he admits that he does not presume to ask for
forgiveness because he knows that he is undeserving of it (*Pa* 253).

---

19 The subtitle of Part Two of the novel, "Boquitas azules, violáceas, negras"
    [Sweet little blue, purplish, black mouths], is an invention of the author and
    stands in sombre, even macabre, contrast to the "Boquitas pintadas de rojo
    carmesí" [Sweet little crimson-painted mouths] of Part One.

20 Claude Le Bigot, "Fantasme, mythe et parole dans *El beso de la mujer araña* de
    Manuel Puig," *Les Langues Néo-Latines* 75.3 (1981): 25–56.

When Herminia (*RH* 280) considers the ballet *Giselle* (1841, music by Adolphe Adam, from a story by Théophile Gautier and Vernoy de Saint-Georges), male deception is indicated on two levels. In *Giselle*, the hero's treachery causes the death of the heroine, but of greater interest is Herminia's preoccupation with the *Wilis*, dead virgins spurned by their prospective bridegrooms, a reference that underlines her view that female fulfilment is possible only through marriage.[21]

The conflict between love and mistrust is recognized by one of the chorus-girls in the film *Ziegfeld Follies* (dir. Vincente Minelli, 1944), which furnishes the epigraph for chapter 10 of *The Buenos Aires Affair*.[22] She confesses that she has been asking herself why "los hombres que queremos no son como queremos" [the men we love are not what we would want them to be] (*BAA* 163). Even though this certainly applies to Leo, Gladys goes on loving him. The hero of *La puerta de oro* (*Hold Back the Dawn*, with Olivia de Havilland, Charles Boyer, and Paulette Goddard, dir. Mitchell Leisen, 1941), the plot of which Toto recounts to Mita (*RH* 138), is also untrustworthy, as is the husband in *The Constant Nymph* (with Joan Fontaine, Charles Boyer, and Alexis Smith, dir. Edmund Goulding, 1943)—a favorite of both Mita and her friend Delia (*RH* 128)—who deserts his wife for a young girl. Exactly the same kind of betrayal takes place in Toto's beloved *The Great Waltz* (with Fernand Gravet, Luise Rainer, and Miliza Korjus, dir. Julien Duvivier, 1938) (*RH* 244 *et seq.*), in *Intermezzo* (with Ingrid Bergman and Leslie Howard, dir. Gregory Ratoff, 1939), and in *The Great Ziegfeld* (with William Powell, Luise Rainer, and Myrna Loy, dir. Robert Z. Leonard, 1936), in which the abandoned wife actually dies. All these plots have peculiar resonances for Puig's female creations. However, although Toto should be seen as one of these, when he re-

---

21 *Giselle* is also mentioned in *Pubis angelical* (92). Here the implication may be that happiness is possible only if the social pressures created by the systematization of human sexuality were diminished. See also chapter VI.

22 In fact, Lana Turner—to whom the most important lines of dialogue are attributed—was not in *Ziegfeld Follies*, but Lucille Ball, whose photograph accompanies the epigraph, was. When I pointed this out to the author, he admitted that he had made this change deliberately, but said that all it revealed was that he preferred Lana Turner (who actually did appear in *Ziegfeld Girl*, with James Stewart, Hedy Lamarr, and Judy Garland, dir. Robert Z. Leonard, 1941) to Lucille Ball.

writes *The Great Ziegfeld* (*RH* 76 *et seq.*) he is still too young to identify with, and enjoy, its tragic elements and he changes the ending. The image of the perfidious male is so common in fiction that Hollywood melodramas often had preposterous plots in an attempt to avoid narrative repetition. The question of credibility at any level is therefore bound to arise. Few were more absurd than *Alma en la sombra* (*Rage in Heaven,* with Robert Montgomery and Ingrid Bergman, dir. W. S. Van Dyke II, 1941), in which an unjustifiably jealous husband arranges his own death in order to implicate his wife's supposed lover (*RH* 139). It is tempting to ask why Puig should have felt that this reference was appropriate in the uneventful context of Coronel Vallejos, until we remember that Berto, Mita's husband, is also prey to ungovernable jealousy.[23] In effect, there are invariably enough recognizable elements in implausibly sentimental plots for audiences or readers to suspend their disbelief. Molina in *El beso de la mujer araña* illustrates this when he leaps to the defense of bolero lyrics, which Valentín has just dismissed as valueless: "Dicen montones de verdades" [There's so much truth in them], he claims, and it is not long before Valentín also identifies with one of them (*Ebma* 143 *et seq.*). The resonances of all levels of art cannot be denied, but any definition of the truth content is bound to be suspect.

One of the author's most original contributions to Post-Boom literature was his conviction that the male need to feel superior harms both sexes: we are made aware of his mixed feelings as he demonstrates that *macho* men are not immune to confusion and frustration. In *Boquitas pintadas,* for example, Juan Carlos struggles ineffectually to be faithful to one woman and to behave like an "hombre de verdad" [real man] (52), but, like Josemar (*Sac*), he is actually incapable of turning his back on the received image of male power and control. Authorial sympathy with this position is confirmed by cultural correlatives throughout the texts. While these underline the proprietorial and manipulative nature of men, as in Molina's narrated version (*Ebma* 163–216) of *I Walked with a Zombie* (with Frances Dee, dir. Jacques

---

23 "Por suerte tu papá no mató al Director del Hospital" [It was only luck that stopped your daddy from killing the hospital director], says the servant-girl, Amparo, to Toto, after one of Berto's jealous rages (*RH* 24).

Tourneur, 1945),[24] or suggest that they are little better than monsters or wild animals—for example, in *Dracula* (with Bela Lugosi, dir. Tod Browning, 1930), or *The Wolf Man* (with Lon Chaney Jr. and Claude Rains, dir. George Waggner, 1940), which, significantly, Molina brackets together with the zombie film—the nature of the intertextual reference is exculpatory. For Molina, and for Puig, the cruel zombie-master is as much a victim as Dracula or the Wolf Man, and they are both as blameless as the *mujer pantera* [panther woman] in the same novel.

Another man whose duality is underlined by means of a cultural reference is Leo in *The Buenos Aires Affair*, who sees the Praxiteles statue of Hermes in his mind's eye (204–05). At this point in the narrative, the reader is already aware that Leo's excessive maleness is an intolerable burden to him, and that his neurosis is caused by an exaggerated need to be in control. He has much in common with Hermes, symbol of ithyphallic force, who, like him, was sexually precocious and pleaded youth and the absence of malicious intent when censured. Given the sinister side of Leo's character, Hermes's connections with the underworld are also relevant, and the existence of maternal incest in his alchemical "Dark Mercurius" aspect is reflected in Leo's excessive devotion to his sister and to María Esther, both surrogate mothers.[25] The nature of the problem, and even a kind of (non-)solution, are indicated in the juxtaposition between the beauty of the male figure and the fact that its oversized phallus is missing. This implied line of reasoning is given added impact when we recall the belief that Hermes engendered a bisexual being, Hermaphroditos,[26] but Leo's defense against any suspicion that there might be alternative behavior patterns for heterosexual men is to indulge in physical and psychological violence, the latter toward a homosexual colleague. As Sharon Magnarelli has observed, "it has rarely occurred to anyone in authority to share that prestige with the powerless group or to make any special effort to improve the image of that other

---

24 The hero's first wife is the only female zombie, since it is scarcely necessary for women to be further incapacitated, but the whole of the zombie workforce could be seen as representing the female sex, as well as other oppressed groups.

25 H.J. Rose, *A Handbook of Greek Mythology* (1928; London: Methuen, 1964) 146–47. C.G. Jung, *Alchemical Studies*, trans. R.F.C. Hull (New York: Bollingen Foundation, 1967) 232.

26 Rose, *Greek Mythology*, 148–49.

group."[27] Leo's sense of authority is fragile indeed, and, like Juan Carlos and Josemar, he feels constrained to make the most strenuous efforts to conserve this.

The superior man is a paradigm for virtually everyone in the Puig novels. *Machismo* and female collusion are not confined to the poor, unintelligent, uneducated, or untalented. Perceptive—and in some cases apparently altruistic—male characters are manipulative exploiters of the opposite sex (Valentín [*Ebma*] and Pozzi [*Pa*] are cases in point), and their behavior is condoned and even admired by women such as Gladys (*BAA*) and Ana (*Pa*), as well as by Molina, the encapsulation of pre-feminist values, who claims that men are "hijos de puta" [sons of bitches] who stick together to conserve their power (*Ebma* 65), but admits that he cannot resist them. That the author treats them all with equal sympathy precludes any determination of a clearcut ideology on his part, and the cross-referring between the narratives and the cultural allusions emphasizes his understanding of his characters and signals his ambivalence.

MADNESS AND DEATH

For Puig's female characters, narratives that focus on the most extreme outcomes of unwarranted suffering have a particular appeal, providing them with a consolatory sense of its inevitability, alleviating feelings of victimized isolation, and suggesting that their own circumstances are relatively tolerable.[28] Insanity and death are accepted as metaphors: exaggerated, but not false, signifiers of recognizable extratextual circumstances. Melodrama's transcendentally heroic mode is also therapeutic in that its grandiose proportions subsume individual situations into a kind of universal epic.[29]

---

27 Magnarelli, *The Lost Rib*, 12.

28 Two Spanish proverbs illustrate different views of this circumstance. Whereas the first, "Mal de muchos, gozo es" [Two in distress makes sorrow less < *Solamen miseris socios habuisse malorum*], reflects the attitude of the Puig characters, the second is more cynical: "Mal de muchos, consuelo de tontos" [Only fools find comfort in general distress].

29 Richard de Cordova designates this "the dramatisation of the private realm." "The Emergence of the Star System and the Bourgeoisification of the American Cinema," *Star Signs* (London: British Film Institute, 1982).

So it is that when fictional love leads to mental derangement, this is not judged implausible, but comforting. (Even in the narrative of Puig's penultimate novel, *Sangre de amor correspondido*, Josemar—as influenced by the myths and devices of fiction as any woman—confidently asserts that Maria da Gloria, the girl he claims to have seduced, lost her mind when he abandoned her.[30]) This situation is indicated throughout Puig's novels by means of the mention of the titles of works of art from several different genres: cinema, the ballet, opera, and the novel. For example, it is safe to assume that Toto and Mita's enjoyment of *Juárez* (with Bette Davis, Brian Aherne, and Paul Muni, dir. William Dieterle, 1939) is not connected with the film's political content, and that they are completely unaware that it was part of a new North American mass media policy toward Latin America;[31] it is, rather, the mad Empress Carlota's unwavering dedication to her dead husband—*amor más allá de la muerte* [love beyond death]—that moves them (*RH* 139). For Mita, it is a plot that clearly demonstrates the ineffable nature of true love, and Herminia's interest in *Giselle*, which has already been referred to, suggests that she shares this view, for here too the betrayed heroine goes mad before dying, but returns from the grave to save her faithless lover's life. It goes without saying that Ana (*Pa*) has always seen love in this way, and this is underlined by passing references to operas that formed part of her sentimental education: Donizetti's *Lucia di Lammermoor* and Bellini's *I Puritani* (*Pa* 95, 165), both of which have heroines who go out of their minds. Another such heroine is Cathy, in Emily Brontë's *Wuthering Heights* (1847), which is mentioned as a novel by Larry (*Me* 48)—significantly, he is so far removed from its emotional orientation that he has never

---

30 This is but one instance of the male-created view that insanity results if female sexual drives are thwarted. For more on this idea, together with a large number of manifestations of its representation in the visual arts, see Bram Dijkstra, *Idols of Perversity: Fantasies of Feminine Evil in Fin-de-Siècle Culture* (New York: Oxford UP, 1986), especially chapter 8. In later years, Hollywood perpetuated this myth, albeit less explicitly and in a watered-down fashion. Commenting on the film *Now, Voyager* (1942)—a favorite of Manuel Puig's—Maria Laplace observes that the heroine "cannot gain her sanity without clear-cut male approval." "Producing and Consuming," 145.

31 This was Hollywood's so-called "Good Neighbor Policy." *Juárez* "offered a panegyric to a nineteenth-century Mexican president and portrayed him as an equal to Abraham Lincoln." Allen L. Woll, *The Latin American Image in American Film* (Los Angeles: UCLA Latin American Center Publ., 1977) 60.

read it—and as a film (with Merle Oberon and Laurence Olivier, dir. William Wyler, 1939) by Toto (*RH* 94), whose only interest in it concerns Cathy's alienation.[32]

Equally striking is the disproportionate number of references to women for whom death is the ineluctable consequence of loving selflessly and honorably. In Delibes' opera *Lakmé* (1883) (*Pa* 68), a young Indian girl gives her life for an unattainable superior man, and it may be that Ana/the *Ama*'s awareness of the possible parallel between this and her own situation is one of the causes of the unease that the music produces. Then, at the end of *The Buenos Aires Affair* when Gladys is contemplating suicide, she realizes that she will miss the performance of an opera that she has always wanted to hear (*BAA* 233). That this is named cannot be without significance: it is Puccini's *Turandot* (1926), in which the hapless Liù, consumed by unrequited love, resists torture and then kills herself.

Although men are sometimes portrayed as the sacrificial victims of overpowering love, this in no way detracts from the feminocentric focus of the allusions: the circumstance adds yet another element of consolation to the impact of romantic melodrama on susceptible women. It not only panders to wishful thinking on the subject of male devotion,[33] but also proves that superior men do exist. In *Il Trovatore*

---

32 The Spanish title, which presumably was chosen in order to emphasize its melodramatic values, was *Cumbres de pasión* [Peaks of Passion], even though the book has always been called *Cumbres borrascosas* in Spanish. In *Cae la noche tropical*, we discover that the Brontës hold so much appeal for the two elderly sisters that they once went on a pilgrimage to the Brontë home in Yorkshire (*Cnt* 31, 33–34).

33 This is also true of the tangos of the thirties, which often portray undying male devotion. One example is "Volver" (1934), by Alfredo LePera and Carlos Gardel, from which the epigraphs to the eighth and sixteenth *entregas* of *Boquitas pintadas* are taken. "Veinte años no es nada" [twenty years are nothing] to the man who is returning to his lost love. Earlier tangos often expressed the genuine longing for love of lone male immigrants to Argentina, but Puig's female characters, such as La Raba (*Bp*), relate to later lyrics, which are much more sentimental and implausible. That they should identify with the words of boleros is more easily explicable. In *El beso de la mujer araña*, Molina (who sees himself as a woman) knows virtually all the Agustín Lara lyrics—one of which also provides the epigraph for the fifteenth *entrega* of *Boquitas pintadas*—and quotes from Mario Clavel's "Mi carta" (*Ebma* 142). In *La tajada* (see above, n. 2), one of the male characters professes scorn for boleros, alleging that they are popular only with homosexuals.

(*RH* 277–78), for example, both the heroine and the hero go to their graves. The lyric of the Roberto Carlos song, which is repeated throughout *Sangre de amor correspondido*, also describes the anguish of both lovers (*Sac* 9–10, 45, 100, 205), thereby underlining Maria da Gloria's (presumed) suffering in Josemar's mind, as well as his own sublimated frustration. Furthermore, the film *Algiers* (with Hedy Lamarr and Charles Boyer, dir. John Cromwell, 1938), which crops up more often than any other cultural paradigm named in Puig's novels (*Bp* 149; *BAA* 45, and as the epigraph to chapter 8; *Pa* 160–61), has a hero who risks, and ultimately loses, his life for the sake of the heroine. For "women's picture" audiences, the depiction of male desperation validates the meek subservience of female models, from the eponymous "great man's lady" to Elisabeth in Wagner's *Tannhäuser* (1845), who prays for death in order to win forgiveness for her lover.[34] At her concert début, Herminia had played the Prelude to *Tannhäuser*[35] (*RH* 269), potentially the beginning of a life of sacrificial love, but for her the whole opera is not to be performed. However, she never loses her faith in male superiority, refusing to question patriarchal norms, and blaming fate—and herself—for her lack of fulfilment. Like all romantic heroines, she disregards the possibility of achieving any kind of "non-normative control," to use Mary Beth Haralovich's term, since happy endings in the type of narrative that influences and reflects the values of all Puig's women are invariably based on romantic love. Wayward heroines must be "recuperated," ceding anything they may have gained.[36]

---

34 Bram Dijkstra (*Idols of Perversity*) associates the cult and model of the self-sacrificing woman (which in protestant Europe was born in the nineteenth century) with the rise of industrialism and trade, and emphasizes "oppressive male sentimentality about the soul-healing power of female virtue" (9), based on the fact that men's own "spiritual responsibility to enrich themselves entailed considerable moral dangers to their immortal souls" (7–8). In countries with a Catholic tradition (the majority of immigrants to Argentina in the early years of this century were either Italian or Spanish), the paradigm of the Virgin Mary also has to be taken into account.

35 It is difficult to avoid recalling Cézanne's painting, "Young Girl at the Piano— Overture to *Tannhäuser*" (c. 1869–70) at this point, but the connection may not have been intended by the author.

36 Mary Beth Haralovich, "Woman's Proper Place: Defining Gender Roles in Film and History," unpublished paper for an independent study with Professor Jeanne Allen, University of Wisconsin–Madison (1979). Quoted by Annette

For obvious reasons, Puig's female creations are most likely to identify with doomed heroines whose only asset is their innocence. In *La traición de Rita Hayworth*, one of the disgruntled Coronel Vallejos girls is reading Galdós's *Marianela* (1878),[37] which Mita describes as "beautiful" (*RH* 181). This allusion differs from most of the others in that the novel's female protagonist is plain, uneducated, untalented, insignificant, and badly dressed. She is no stranger to suffering (her mother committed suicide), and she lives in unattractive surroundings that are not all that far removed from the ugly aridity of small towns in the Argentine Pampa. The one man with whom she manages to establish an affective bond is blind, but when an operation restores his sight he abandons her in favor of his beautiful cousin and she dies of a broken heart.[38] Nobody, it seems, is to blame, but if this is so the only conclusion that can be drawn is that life and fate are cruelly unfair.

Now it may, and should, be objected that women are far more likely to be victims than men. To a later generation it seems obvious that women like Marianela (and Puig's female creations) should not indulge in masochistic surrender to their supposed impotence and lack of beauty, since this attitude actually serves to decrease their power and may lead to the suffering that is signified in melodrama by alienation and death. That the author was conscious of this is suggested by the fact that in *The Buenos Aires Affair* there are references to films that portray women who deal with loss in different ways: alcoholism, resignation, and, in one case, a kind of "non-normative control," which nevertheless springs from undying love. They constitute possible paradigms

---

Kuhn in *Women's Pictures: Feminism and Cinema* (London: Routledge, 1982) 34. "Recuperated" is Kuhn's word.

37 The fact that Galdós has never enjoyed great popularity in Latin America confirms the very conscious process of selection of cultural references on the part of the author. It is extremely unlikely that *Marianela* would have been typical reading matter for the inhabitants of General Villegas.

38 The only example in a Puig text of a submissive, virtuous, *and plain* woman who finds love is Molina's version of *The Enchanted Cottage* (with Dorothy McGuire and Robert Young, dir. John Cromwell, 1945)—though the film's title is not actually given. By means of this, Molina signals the parallel between the heroine's misleading plainness and his own appearance, which—since he does not see himself as a man—is equally misleading. In this case, too, there is a blind character who is misled by external factors, but this is as much a question of wishful thinking as is Ana's belief in a superior man.

for Gladys (abandoned by Leo, who then dies) and her mother, Clara Evelia, who, though full of self-pity because she has been widowed, is trying to establish a new life for herself.[39] As in Ana's self-projections in *Pubis angelical*, none of the role models furnishes a solution. Clara Evelia goes on hating her daughter and resenting the demands she makes, torn between the need to live up to the image of the sacrificial mother and her desire for independence. As for Gladys, her last action in the text is to take a sleeping pill and withdraw from life.

Injustice and suffering are evident both in the lives of the heroines of Puig's novels and of those alluded to in the second fictions, who closely reflect their situations. However, once again there is a notable absence of ideology with regard to this topic. The superior man and faith in love as the reward for female virtue and pain may well be illusions—beliefs "motivated by a wish-fulfilment which sets no store by verification from reality," as Freud defined the term[40]—but it is difficult to discern *from the texts* a world view that would be preferable. Although the author enthusiastically espoused various forms of social change in his many interviews,[41] his novels indicate that he saw both sides of even the most loaded questions.

---

39 In *Mañana lloraré* (*I'll Cry Tomorrow*, with Susan Hayward and Richard Conte, dir. Daniel Mann, 1955), an alcoholic woman is masochistically determined to remember her dead lover (epigraph to chapter 9): the heroine's wilful determination to suffer echoes Gladys's obsession with Leo. The inscrutable Greta Garbo faces up to the death of her lover in *Grand Hotel* (with Greta Garbo and John Barrymore, dir. Edmund Goulding, 1932), as Gladys is also obliged to do (*BAA* 45, and epigraph to chapter 15). However, *Tierna camarada* (*Tender Comrade*, with Ginger Rogers and Robert Ryan, dir. Edward Dmytryk, 1943) reflects the self-perception of Clara Evelia, since it is the story of a courageous widow struggling to bring up a baby alone (*BAA* 45 and epigraph to chapter 14).

40 Sigmund Freud, "The Future of an Illusion," (1927) *Standard Edition of the Complete Psychological Works of Sigmund Freud*, trans. and ed. James Strachey, in collaboration with Anna Freud, 24 vols. (London: Hogarth and Institute of Psycho-analysis) 21: 31. In future notes the *Standard Edition* will be referred to as *SE*.

41 For example, in an unpublished interview in 1987, the author told me that he had "a new theory" that was based on the removal of any moral implications from sexual behavior. (This was not, of course, new, but reflected the Freudo-Marxist ideology of the sixties.) He then met all my objections by pointing out that total sexual freedom, unrelated to love and loyalty, had not yet been tried, and could not therefore be dismissed.

WOMAN THE BETRAYER

In spite of so many secondary indications to the contrary, Puig's narratives never portray men as invincible. The author frequently underlines male debility, signalling the marginality of Molina in *El beso de la mujer araña* and even revealing sympathy for *macho* and despotic characters in other texts.[42] (The latter element is usually ignored by his critics.) A sign of his non-prescriptive understanding of the male (and, perhaps, homosexual) condition is his utilization of cultural references to the *femme fatale* stereotype and to treacherous mothers. However, these are important for another reason: since both images come from the male imagination, they suggest danger and unhappiness for both sexes.

It has often been asserted that men's will to power is based on a deep-rooted fear of women—that is, fear of the ultimately uncontrollable. This may come from sexual attraction, which can subjugate and even destroy; or from the archetype of the Terrible Mother, who annihilates as well as creates; or, in Catholic societies, from the risk of abandonment, disillusion, and loss, should the myth of the protective, immaculate mother crumble. In all cases, woman is also mystery, embodying the unknown and the unknowable, and the fear that she provokes may well turn into hatred. As Freud observed, hatred "always remains in an intimate relation with the self-preservative instincts."[43] In order to provide themselves with a sense of security—for myth is essentially a defense mechanism—men have always divided women into two polarized categories: the (good) mother and the (bad) whore, but this stratagem does not succeed in eradicating either subconscious fear of the Archetypal Feminine, or the possibility of the collapse of a social and psychological stereotype.

In the iconography of the Archetypal Feminine, positive and negative aspects are inextricably linked. If archetypes are absolutes, male apprehension is justified and male ambivalence underlined; as Theodor Reik has pointed out (and it is difficult to disagree), "the first myths [were] produced by, and meant for, men."[44] Resulting behavior pat-

---

42 For example, Berto (*RH*), Juan Carlos (*Bp*), Leo (*BAA*), and Josemar (*Sac*), all of whom had expectations that were not realized.

43 Freud, "Instincts and their Vicissitudes," *SE* 4 (1915).

44 Theodor Reik, *The Creation of Woman* (New York: McGraw-Hill, 1960) 17.

terns involve exploitation and abuse, which are explicable in terms of male resistance to the sinister side of female sexuality. There is no shortage of anecdotal evidence for this stance in the arts, where women are invariably quasi-divine or dangerous.

The Young Witch, the seductive and treacherous half of the dichotomy, can—like Circe—turn men into beasts unless she is controlled or eliminated.[45] The drive for self-preservation is therefore the basis for men's struggle for hegemony, and their attitude is vindicated by the fact that the women will be redeemed by control, and will redeem them in turn.[46] It might be argued that the means of redemption should be love, but if this does exist, it is subordinate to male attempts at ego-preservation. In fiction, transgressing females suffer and die as frequently as their more virtuous sisters.

Nevertheless, there are several allusions in Puig's novels to predatory females who cannot be tamed. The most obvious example, perhaps, is the siren figure played by Rita Hayworth in *Blood and Sand* (also starring Tyrone Power, dir. Rouben Mamoulian, 1941).[47] In the movie, based on Vicente Blasco Ibáñez's novel *Sangre y arena* (1909), the irresistible doña Sol lures a young bullfighter from the path of righteousness, ultimately bringing about his death, while she herself emerges unscathed from this act of treachery. Although Sharon Magnarelli is right to claim that the hero of the novel was always an indifferent *matador*, betrayed less by doña Sol than by his own "pride, arrogance, and self-delusions,"[48] this is not emphasized in the film; here audiences of both sexes will judge his downfall to be the fault of

---

45 See Erich Neumann, *The Great Mother: An Analysis of the Archetype*, trans. Ralph Manheim, 2nd ed. (Princeton: Princeton UP, 1963), especially the chapters, "The Positive Elementary Character" and "The Negative Elementary Character" (chapters 10 and 11).

46 Neumann, *The Great Mother*, 74, 75, 77, 289, 295, 35.

47 Rita Hayworth often played similar roles, and the epigraph to chapter 16 of *The Buenos Aires Affair* is taken from *Gilda* (also starring Glenn Ford, dir. Charles Vidor, 1946), in which she was a seductive, but this time innocent, *femme fatale*. It is a good example of male fear of being diminished by a desirable woman turning into odium. (Richard Winnington, in a brief assessment of the film, mentions the "words of hate" that permeate the dialogue. Quoted by Leslie Halliwell, *Halliwell's Film Guide*, 2nd ed. [London: Granada, 1982] 408). Needless to say, the hero's attitude echoes that of Leo in the novel.

48 Magnarelli, *The Lost Rib*, 141–42.

an inherently evil woman. Among the many explanations of the "betrayal of Rita Hayworth" in Puig's first novel,[49] it is the most obvious and literal one that is relevant in this context.

Jean Harlow was another actress who invariably embodied uncontrollable sexual danger, and two of her films are mentioned in the course of the texts. The first is *Saratoga* (also starring Clark Gable, dir. Jack Conway, 1937), which is being shown in Buenos Aires when Mabel is staying there (*Bp* 140). The other, *Dinner at Eight* (with John Barrymore and Wallace Beery, dir. George Cukor, 1933), is used as the epigraph to chapter 5 of *The Buenos Aires Affair*. The Jean Harlow character furnishes an exaggerated role model for both Mabel and Gladys, both of whom are different from their contemporaries in that they have actually broken the rules and indulged in premarital sexual activity. In the event, neither manages to reconcile her emancipated behavior, and the scant amount of non-normative control that she achieves, with her romantic aspirations. Liberation has not worked for them. In *The Buenos Aires Affair*, the epigraph to chapter 11 highlights the danger to men of female power as a not-so-Young Witch callously watches her husband die; this is taken from the film *The Little Foxes* (with Bette Davis and Herbert Marshall, dir. William Wyler, 1941). Again it is a question of female collusion, as women, repelled by male-created stereotypes—the Spanish title of *The Little Foxes* was *La loba* [The She-Wolf][50]—are driven further into conforming roles.

There are two more instances of invincible, combatant women that merit attention. The first is the heroine of *A caza de novio* (*Her Cardboard Lover*, with Norma Shearer and Robert Taylor, dir. George Cukor, 1941), who hires a man to make her fiancé jealous. According to Toto, the film is "lovely" and "glamorous" (*RH* 92), and it may be judged innocuous escapist pleasure for the inhabitants of Coronel Vallejos, which is neither. Furthermore, it is only a film, and, because of the Great Divide between highbrow culture and mass art, its

---

49 These include the untrustworthy nature of beauty, the dawning realization on the part of Toto that he is incapable of being a carbon-copy of his *macho* father, Berto's own thwarted ambitions, and Mita's double-dealing between Toto's world and that of the adults. See my *The Necessary Dream*, chapter 1; Piglia, "Clase media: cuerpo y destino"; Evelyne Minard, "*La traición de Rita Hayworth*: violence et mort dans l'Argentine de Manuel Puig," *Cahiers du Monde Hispanique et Luso-Brésilien* 39 (1982): 75–80.

50 Cf. Molina's *Wolf Man* in *El beso de la mujer araña*.

values—or those of any of the cinematic products referred to—have never been judged worthy of investigation or comment. Yet it is important, for its plot again revolves around deception and recourse to underhand stratagems on the part of a woman pursuing power; its effect is ambiguous, as it undermines the concept of female moral superiority, which a contemporary audience would wish to conserve, while allowing the heroine to achieve her goal.

Scarlett O'Hara in *Gone with the Wind* (with Vivien Leigh and Clark Gable, dir. Victor Fleming, George Cukor, and Sam Wood, 1939), is another heroine who is fundamentally unscathed by circumstances. At the end of the film—and of Margaret Mitchell's novel—she is thinking about her future; she has not been controlled, much less destroyed. The work merits only a passing mention in *La traición de Rita Hayworth* (83), and even that is concerned only with the costumes, so that it may appear that there is little to be gained by investigating it, but the fact that it is named at all has to be borne in mind. At the very least, it means that Toto and his circle have seen it and have assimilated some of its messages. One of these may be that immunity from suffering at the hands of men is won only by means of "unfeminine" callousness and disregard for the (patriarchal) rules. In the lives of Mabel and Gladys (who, as a child, could not achieve a likeness of Vivien Leigh in a drawing), attempts at independence of spirit or behavior prove self-defeating. Erring women must be recuperated or they will be ostracized.

Turandot, the eponymous heroine of the opera referred to in *The Buenos Aires Affair*, is a striking example of recuperation. She is a princess who has offered her hand to any man who can answer three riddles; those who fail are executed. When Prince Calaf answers them correctly, she adds faithlessness to cruelty by refusing to be his. His response is to offer to forfeit his life if she can guess his name, immediately volunteering the information himself. Audiences almost certainly attribute this to his overpowering love for Turandot,[51] but an alternative interpretation is that he is prepared to risk everything to eliminate a challenge to male power. His overweening confidence is vindicated: when he admits that she has won, she announces to an expectant multitude that his name is Love. The key to power—

---

51 A recent review of a performance of the opera talks of the heroine "melting into womanhood in the final scene." Robert Croan, *Pittsburgh Post-Gazette* (1 February 1991).

women's need for love—had always been in his hands. Indeed, Erich Neumann sees this kind of "trial by the Feminine" as indicative of the relative innocuousness of the Young Witch, for although "the numerous princesses who present riddles to be solved do . . . kill their unsuccessful suitors . . . they do so only in order to give themselves willingly to the victor, whose superiority, shown by his solving of the riddle, redeems the princess herself, who is this riddle."[52] Ultimately, Turandot adopts a normative role via love, and this illustrates Puig's view of the impossible choice faced by Gladys, and all women, within the patriarchy: clearsightedness leads to loveless isolation, while opting for romantic love is synonymous with the acceptance of male domination. Gladys, of course, does not die at the end of *The Buenos Aires Affair*, and there is no reason why she should not see *Turandot*. If she does, she will discover that the plot furnishes an ironic commentary on her own situation, for, like Galdós's Marianela, she is neither beautiful nor powerful. She strayed from normative behavior patterns, starting a career and enjoying a certain success, but in her case love redeemed no one and there was no happy ending. Liù is the only character with whom she could possibly identify.

Expiatory renunciation on the part of the transgressive woman can also be redemptive.[53] Carla in *The Great Waltz*—which impressed Toto (*RH*) so much—returns to the path of virtue by feigning indifference toward her married lover.[54] The nobility of this gesture is proof of the true depth of her emotion, and order is restored—both to the fictional world, as her erstwhile lover, himself now redeemed, returns to his wife, and to the unsettled moral judgments of the audience. The male-created collective superego is served, the erring woman is under control, and at the same time the myth of female virtue survives intact as the man's soul is saved. This paradigmatic process is also indirectly indicated to Ana (*Pa* 165) by means of a passing reference to Massenet's opera *Manon* (1884), in which the wayward heroine dies in a state of loving repentance.

52　Neumann, *The Great Mother*, 35.

53　A sign that Toto's *macho* cousin, Héctor, has not yet reached the stage where his redemption is an important issue is that he despises women's pictures and prefers those that feature glamorous sex symbols (*RH* 160).

54　For a very thorough analysis of *The Great Waltz* and its relevance for Toto, see Campos, *Espejos*, 90 *et seq.*

Such tales of thwarted women are the source of a perverse kind of pleasure for their own sex. This reaction is evident in Toto's wish to be told the story of the film *Intermezzo* over and over again, and the feminization of Valentín reaches its peak when he claims that the tragic ending of Molina's Mexican film is "lo mejor de la película" [the best part of the movie] (*Ebma* 263). In general, they are sustained by the belief that love is impervious to hostile circumstances, even if happiness is shortlived.[55] The logic behind this reaction is somewhat difficult to discern: in eternal triangles such as the one portrayed in *The Great Waltz*, both the neglected wife and the (wicked) mistress truly love the hero. One answer may be that whereas Turandot is initially two-dimensional, apparently symbolizing unadulterated evil,[56] and attains virtue only through salvation, morally ambiguous models embody the impossible choices that all human beings are obliged to confront. Another is that, unlike actual experience, fictional examples of shortlived happiness confirm the very existence of overwhelming love.[57] A third, which emphasizes the correlation between many a *femme fatale* and evil, is the conditioned view that virtuous women are asexual, and that a grand passion must not be consummated. In romantic melodramas, the flesh is comfortably spiritualized. This attitude is underlined on several occasions: for example, in *La traición de Rita Hayworth*, when Delia confesses to weeping during the showing of *The Constant Nymph*, but immediately reveals how repulsive she finds the sexual advances of the man she is to marry (*RH* 129); the juxtaposition cannot be fortuitous. Then Mabel's dream is a visit from either Robert Taylor or Tyrone Power—actors who always played "gentle" roles—carrying a bunch of roses, but a "designio voluptuoso" [voluptuous plan] would be discernible in their eyes (*Bp* 140–41).

Maternal betrayal is another constant in Puig's novels. Molina's (invented) terrorist film (*Ebma* 128 *et seq.*) is a cultural reference that mirrors Valentín's political background, but it also highlights his cell-

---

55 *Intermezzo* was called *Escape to Happiness* in Great Britain.

56 Her cruelty was a form of revenge against all men because of an ancestor who was raped. This, of course, tends to cloud the issue and may give rise to further interpretation based on the lust/love dichotomy.

57 Denis de Rougemont has claimed that "the spontaneous ardour of a love crowned and not thwarted is essentially of short duration." *Passion and Society*, trans. Montgomery Belgion (1956; London: Faber, 1962) 45.

mate's disillusioned estrangement from his mother,[58] it is significant
that Molina himself is beginning to question the pernicious effects of
his filial devotion. On a narrative level, in *Maldición eterna a quien lea
estas páginas* Larry alleges that Ramírez's son was disenchanted by his
mother's loyalty to her husband, and in *Sangre de amor correspondido* at
least some of Josemar's problems stem from his refusal to question the
concept of maternal virtue. Clearly, what fails here is a male myth; it
is traumatic for men if it is undermined, but it is always intolerably
oppressive for women. In *Pubis angelical*, Ana's equivocal attitude
toward her daughter causes her much pain, and in the opening chapter
of *The Buenos Aires Affair*, we meet Clara Evelia, a mother whose
feelings toward Gladys are in stark opposition to the maternal ideal.
She actually hopes that her missing daughter is dead, and a contrapun-
tal intertextual allusion, a Bécquer poem that runs unbidden through
her head, clarifies her attitude for the reader. Its subject is the death of
a young girl, and as Clara Evelia tries to recall the lines in question,
she substitutes, "de la pobre niña / *a solas* me acuerdo" [*all alone* I
remember the poor child] for "de la pobre niña / a veces me acuerdo"
[sometimes I remember the poor child] (*BAA* 11). There is no doubting
her resentment in the face of the continual sacrifices she is expected to
make. She cannot, of course, allow herself to face up to her feelings,
and the message from her superego is summed up in the elusive ending to the poem, which points out that there is "algo que repugna"
[something repugnant] in abandoning the dead to isolation.[59]

At first it appears that both intertextual examples of men's fear of
female sexuality and narrative and referential instances of misplaced
faith in immaculate mothers suggest a demythifying purpose on the
part of the author, yet his equivocal attitude is also evident. Even if
they are being duped, none of his characters is condemned, or even
made to look foolish, and Puig reveals his fascination for the works of
art that influence them in the specificity and frequency of their
appearance in his texts. It is never clear whether he judges these as
perniciously manipulative or whether, like Molina's boleros, their
appeal lies in the fact that there is so much truth in them. Like all
postmodern writers, he was a stranger to certainty.

---

58 Puig himself maintained on several occasions that political and psychosexual
oppression were inextricably linked.

59 Gustavo Adolfo Bécquer (1836–70), *Rima* 73.

II

The Female Image

MATERNAL SACRIFICE

ALTHOUGH THE CULT of the mother is not restricted to Catholic
countries, it is in these that Marian veneration has always given rise
to "the mythology that motherhood is the central point of a woman's
life," to quote Marina Warner.[1] So it is that in Puig's Argentina, with
its tradition of maternal reverence,[2] any narrative that focuses on and
perpetuates such a paradigm will be particularly well received.

Yet, as we have seen, Clara Evelia's troubled hostility toward
Gladys (*BAA*) is an extreme example of the impossibility of emulating
the sacrificial purity, devotion, and humility of the Virgin. She finds
herself in an impossible position, unable to resist the pressures of an
idealism that is largely the result of socio-religious conditioning, but

---

1 Marina Warner, *Alone of All Her Sex: The Myth and Cult of the Virgin Mary*
   (London: Weidenfeld and Nicolson, 1976) 284.

2 This is manifest in several areas of Argentine mass culture; for example, one of
   the principal themes of the tango is the saintly mother, representing what
   Noemí Ulla calls "la bondad suburbana" [virtue in the slums]. Noemí Ulla,
   Tango, rebelión y nostalgia (Buenos Aires: Editorial Jorge Alvarez, 1967) 45. "Sólo
   una madre nos perdona en esta vida" [Only a mother will forgive us in this
   life], we find in "La casita de los viejos" (lyric by Enrique Cadícamo, date unknown); "Madre hay una sola" [You have only one mother] is the title of a
   tango by José de la Vega (1930); and the narrator of the well-known "Adiós,
   muchachos" (lyric by César A. Vedoni, 1927) recalls the good times spent with
   his mother, a "santa viejita" [saintly little old lady].

that can also be attributed to the sublimation of internal drives. Molly Haskell has claimed that obsessive and masochistic maternal love (or, in Clara Evelia's case, the appeal of this concept) is the masked expression of sexual frustration,[3] and the kind of society investigated by Manuel Puig is peopled by women whose romantic illusions have been dashed and for whom their sexuality is a taboo topic. They therefore turn their attention elsewhere and find some consolation in the rightness of the maternal role: after all, as Marina Warner says, "the natural order for the female sex [has been] ordained as motherhood." Furthermore, a certain (normative) power is acquired, since in such societies "the idea that a woman might direct matters in her own right is not even entertained."[4] Theoretically, therefore, this displacement of vital female energies within the patriarchy promises a certain fulfilment, if not happiness.

However, happiness, far from being assured, is elusive. Clara Evelia is not the only Puig mother disturbed and confused by the difficulty of living up to the demands of her role: Mita (*RH*), for example, is disappointed in her son, feeling that the baby who died would have been all that the effeminate Toto is not. (As René Alberto Campos has noted, her utopian ideal is a son who would be "masculino y sensible a la vez" [male and sensitive at the same time], as personified by Hollywood leading men.[5]) But it is in *The Buenos Aires Affair* that the largest number of secondary references to maternal sacrifice is found.[6] Clara Evelia's role models are intertextually present in epigraphs taken from Hollywood films, by means of which the author indicates mandatory behavior patterns. First (chapter 3), there is *El suplicio de una madre* [A Mother's Agony]—a much more significant title than the English original (*Mildred Pierce*, with Joan Crawford, dir. Michael Curtiz, 1945)—in which Puig very deliberately focuses on the stormy relationship between a self-sacrificing lone woman and her snobbish ingrate of a daughter. Since the film was far more concerned with the perils of female independence—the heroine was alone because she had

---

3   Molly Haskell, *From Reverence to Rape: The Treatment of Women in the Movies* (Harmondsworth: Penguin, 1979) 168–70.

4   Warner, *Alone of All Her Sex*, 289.

5   Campos, *Espejos*, 81.

6   Motherhood also features in *Cae la noche tropical*, but here the emphasis is on the passage of time, change, and loss.

deserted her husband—the author's concentration on this minor aspect of it is not without interest. Then (chapter 6), there is *Corazón a corazón* (*Blossoms in the Dust*, with Greer Garson and Walter Pidgeon, dir. Mervyn Le Roy, 1941), in which a widow who has lost her only child bravely and altruistically gives away an orphan to whom she has become attached. As Molly Haskell has observed, those who identified with this heroine were encouraged to "accept, rather then reject, their lot."[7] Lastly (chapter 14), there is *Tierna Camarada* (*Tender Comrade*), in which the widowed Ginger Rogers is admirably stoic and dignified and thinks only of the future of her child. All these allusions make a mother's duty incontrovertibly clear.

It is not just a question of the fact—as Molly Haskell views it—that the inviolability of the maternal ethos constitutes a barrier to any improvement in the status of women; the fallibility of the ethos itself must also be taken into consideration. Theory/desire and (uncontrollable) practice are invariably at odds, as is indirectly echoed in Clara Evelia's vigorous declamation of Gabriela Mistral's poem "Esterilidad" [Sterility] when she feels most betrayed by Gladys (*BAA* 32). One of Gabriela Mistral's principal themes was childlessness,[8] and in comparison with the ideal, Clara Evelia sees herself as childless too. Gladys constantly humiliates and isolates her by failing to play her part in a paradigmatic, but fictitious, relationship.

All the narratives contain confused, even disillusioned, mothers. Choli, Mita's friend (*RH*), is repelled by what she sees as her son's coarse masculinity; Nené (*Bp*) finds her two boys singularly unprepossessing; and Ana (*Pa*) actually abandons her daughter, another child who has refused to play her part. Maternal disenchantment is also implied, if not portrayed, in the cases of Juan Carlos (*Bp*), Molina (*Ebma*), Larry (*Me*), and Josemar (*Sac*),[9] and in *Cae la noche tropical*,

---

7 Haskell, *From Reverence to Rape*, 155.

8 This is one of many indications that the epoch in which the novels are set is of importance. Gabriela Mistral (Chile, 1889–1957) has been described as "standing between two epochs. Her formation was nineteenth-century. She was a woman of hearth, children, of religious faith. But she was forced to live in a modern world." Jean Franco, *A Literary History of Spain: Spanish American Literature since Independence* (London: Ernest Benn, 1973) 176.

9 It is suggested that Larry, who lives in New York where traditional values are less likely to be observed, was thrown out of the family home by his mother, and in rural Brazil, where these are still upheld, Josemar's mother tires of his

Silvia is saddened by the fact that her son has gone to live in a foreign country and never contacts her. In the maternal context, as well as in the amorous, the alternatives for women are depicted as daunting: acceptance of the social stereotype so forcibly depicted in the cultural allusions will not only inhibit personal fulfilment but will also lead to disillusion, but to challenge this invites destructive feelings of guilt, if not social ostracism.

Puig, of course, advocates neither, and his treatment of maternal figures is yet another manifestation of his absence of self-certainty. Even at the end of *Pubis angelical*, when Ana's resolve to face up to the *reality* of motherhood could be judged a positive change, one made against a background of Lacanian theory (*Pa* 89, 170 *et seq.*), the outcome is far from secure. Her decision to abandon her quest for a superior man could be seen as a kind of second Lacanian mirror-stage of self-knowledge, a repetition of that moment when, as a small child, she first recognized her own integrated reflection. However, like Molina (*Ebma*), she makes her decision *faute de mieux*, and even in the mirror-stage proper, "the image in which we . . . recognize ourselves is a misrecognition."[10] Since, according to Lacan, life itself is desire in progress, distinguished by unending lack which the subject constantly attempts to satisfy with metonymic predicates, Ana's situation is less promising than might at first appear to be the case. It is true that she is not just returning to her mother, which could mean unhealthy regression, and as she once again forms part of the symbolic order there is at least the possibility of a fruitful bond with her daughter; ultimately, though, she is yet another heroine recuperated by the patriarchy (going from one prison to another) who has made a choice between two evils. In Julia Kristeva's view, motherhood is "the material basis for women's oppression."[11]

---

childlike dependence and idleness.

10 Jacques Lacan, quoted in Juliet Mitchell and Jacqueline Rose (eds.), *Feminine Sexuality: Jacques Lacan and the École Freudienne*, trans. Jacqueline Rose (London: Macmillan, 1982) 30. The French term, which is so much more revealing, is *méconnaissance*.

11 See Toril Moi, *Sexual/Textual Politics* (London: Methuen, 1985) 30.

ABUSED WOMEN

Although the complaisance of Puig's female characters regarding fictional examples of ill-fated, abused women is based on their faith in virtue as its own reward, it would be wrong to suggest that the texts contain no cultural references to those few who do achieve happiness. These instances add to the perceived desirability of passivity, for the innocence of the role model is a constant. Laura in *The Enchanted Cottage* (*Ebma*) (the plot of which Molina recounts to himself), finds love against all odds, and in several films (such as *The Great Ziegfeld* [*RH*]), long-suffering wives regain their erring husbands. In Molina's idiosyncratic version of *Cat People* (with Simone Simon, Kent Smith, Tom Conway, and Jane Randolph, dir. Jacques Tourneur, 1942), the hero's female colleague wins his love after previously settling for chaste friendship. This modification of her original film role as his mistress underlines the therapeutic value of the stereotype for Molina,[12] for whom her situation has idealistic resonances even though he actually identifies with the eponymous heroine's lack of control over her sexuality.[13]

Given the type-casting star system of the heyday of Hollywood, ill-used women tended to be played by a relatively small group of actresses. The implications are therefore only too clear when we are told that one of Mita's favorite movies is *Hold Back the Dawn*, which starred one of these, Olivia de Havilland, and that the teacher preferred by Toto is Sister Clara, who has "la cara buena de Olivia de Havilland" [Olivia de Havilland's virtuous features] (*RH* 80).[14]

We are also reminded of the correlation between virtue and suffering by means of a subtle allusion in *Pubis angelical*. In the section that represents Ana's possible future—or, perhaps, that of her

---

12 Maryse Vich-Campos, in "L'invention de Molina (à propos du film *Cat People* dans *El beso de la mujer araña*, de Manuel Puig)," *Actes du Colloque sur l'Oeuvre de Puig et Vargas Llosa. Avril 1982* (Fontenay aux Roses: Les Cahiers de Fontenay, 1982) 107–13, lists and analyzes all the changes made by Molina.

13 Jane Randolph's is the only name actually mentioned by Molina.

14 She also went from humiliation to death in *Gone with the Wind* (*RH*). Although not referred to by Puig, *In This Our Life* (dir. John Huston, 1942) is almost certainly the most striking example of the type-casting of both Olivia de Havilland and her co-star, Bette Davis.

daughter—W218 goes to a fancy-dress ball dressed as Columbine, a gentle character who is always seen in terms of her relationship with the irresponsible, unprincipled, abusive Harlequin. The name Columbine means "dove-like," and it connotes innocent motherhood (a connection reinforced by Ana's own name, which recalls the mother of the Virgin), Venus, and all victims of deception.[15] That she wears a beauty-spot to the ball is also worth noting: the Spanish word *lunar*, connected to the moon, suggests passivity, a tendency toward self-sacrifice, arbitrary fantasizing and imaginative impressionability, all of which are essential elements in the attitude of submissive women.[16]

The *sine qua non* of this role model is spirituality. There is never any question of sexual fulfilment, even though the relationships the woman strives to preserve, including the state of motherhood, are sexually based. Good women are pure women. Toto adores the asexual films of Fred Astaire and Ginger Rogers (*RH* 37, 39, 48), is equally taken with *Romeo and Juliet* (with Norma Shearer and Leslie Howard, dir. George Cukor, 1936),[17] and is impressed by the bland Nelson

---

15 José Luis Morales y Marín, *Diccionario de iconología y simbología* (Madrid: Taurus, 1984) 55, 254.

16 Juan-Eduardo Cirlot, *Diccionario de símbolos* (Barcelona, Editorial Labor, 1969) 85, 159, 297. This motif crops up on two other occasions. One is when the most beautiful whore in a Vietnamese brothel is described as having (natural) *lunares* and a withered breast (*Me* 82). The other, when Molina thinks that the *lunar* on Valentín's face has been transferred to his own after sexual intercourse (*Ebma* 222). The first example may signify potential motherhood blighted by unbridled sexual activity; in any case, the two motifs are obviously defects. The second is even more difficult to interpret, though the transfer obviously suggests fusion. I cannot accept Maurice Molho's view that the *lunar* is a symbol of the penis, given the usual implications of the image, even if Molina does refer to "el lunar . . . que no tengo" [the mole . . . I don't have]. (Maurice Molho, "Tango de la madre araña," *Actes du Colloque sur l'Oeuvre de Puig et Vargas Llosa. Avril 1982* [Fontenay aux Roses: Les Cahiers de Fontenay, 1982] 167.) It may be that Molina's penchant for sacrificial passivity has just been reinforced; alternatively, the fact that it is Valentín who actually has a *lunar* may indicate that he is basically bisexual.

17 In *Boquitas pintadas*, Puig—apparently gratuitously—mentions the "casqueta Julieta" [Juliet cap] that is referred to in one of Mabel's magazines (*Bp* 48). This is in contrast to the sex manuals that she also reads. Conversely, in *La traición de Rita Hayworth*, Héctor's favorite reading matter is the *Kama Sutra* (*RH* 160), which is male-oriented and practical: in the original Sanskrit, the word "karma" admits no distinction between love and sensual gratification, and, by and large,

Eddy/Jeanette MacDonald partnership.[18] His mother reads *Paul et Virginie* by Bernardin de Saint-Pierre (1787), an idyll in which the lovers are little more than children, and it is a short step to protagonists who actually are children. One of these is Shirley Temple—aptly described by René Alberto Campos as "an icon of goodness"[19]—who, after restoring order to the world with her beatific innocence, is invariably rewarded with undemanding love.[20] She seems to be the ideal model for Toto in his attempt to win the affection of his father. Moreover, both he and the adult female characters will have been inspired by the happy ending to the story of another prepubertal icon, Snow White (*Snow White and the Seven Dwarfs*, Walt Disney, 1937) (*RH* 33, 38). Perhaps the ambivalent Mabel in *Boquitas pintadas* should have taken the opportunity to see *La casta Susana* (*La Chaste Suzanne*, with Henri Garat, Meg Lemonnier, and Luise Rainer, 1938) when it was being shown in Buenos Aires,[21] although a more appropriate title from the list that she consults is *No se puede tener todo*

---

the book emphasizes the subordination of women, who are advised to profit from male pleasure.

18 Although not stated specifically, it is likely that "the cabin in the snowy woods," which Toto sees as a refuge from all his problems in the *Familienroman* that he constructs around the plot of *The Great Ziegfeld*, comes from *Rose Marie* (dir. W. S. Van Dyle II, 1936). See Campos, *Espejos*, 68. In *New Moon* (dir. Robert Z. Leonard, 1940), Nelson Eddy and Jeanette MacDonald find themselves in a cabin, which, while tropical rather than Arctic, is also situated in Utopia. *Rose Marie* was so successful in Argentina that a Buenos Aires cinema was named after it; this is mentioned in *Boquitas pintadas*, and, ironically, the film that is being shown there when Mabel consults the program is *Saratoga*, starring the unrepentant sex-symbol Jean Harlow (*Bp* 140).

19 Campos, *Espejos*, 47.

20 According to Campos (*Espejos*, 48), Toto is thinking of *The Little Colonel* (dir. David Butler, 1935) when he remembers how Shirley Temple captivated her irascible grandfather (*RH* 44–45), but the same circumstances obtain in *Heidi* (dir. Allan Dwan, 1937). Another Shirley Temple film that might have served as a *Familienroman* model for Toto (though it is not mentioned) is *Stowaway* (dir. William A. Seiter, 1936), in which an orphan's cheerful optimism in the middle of a Chinese revolution results in her adoption by a rich and affectionate couple.

21 The eponymous heroine's biblical namesake is, of course, another icon of virtue.

(*You Can't Have Everything*, with Alice Faye and Don Ameche, dir. Norman Taurog, 1937) (*Bp* 140).[22]

The curious female ideal that combines asexual love and motherhood can be attributed, like the maternal cult itself, to the Church. As Marina Warner has noted, it is not just nobility that must be striven after:

> At one level, the purpose of woman and her fulfilment is seen to be motherhood, but at another the teleological argument is cut across by a major reservation, expressed succinctly in Canon Ten of the Council of Trent's twenty-fourth session: "virginity and celibacy are better and more blessed than the bond of matrimony" (*Melius ac beatus quam jungi in matrimonio*).

Mary's virgin motherhood has been "the chief sign of her supernatural nature since the sixth century, when the marvellous *Akathistos* hymn hailed her as the one creature in whom all opposites are reconciled"[23]—a disturbing model indeed.

Clearly, all ideal figures are impossible to emulate, but society demands an attempt to do just this, with high moral standards indicated by inflexible behavior patterns. In fiction, this particular stereotype is always dignified and restrained. We have already considered examples of the admirable composure of distressed mothers such as those played by Joan Crawford, Greer Garson, and Ginger Rogers; even in the relationship between men and women, the same rules apply. All women are potential madonnas. The blameless nightclub singer in Molina's (invented) Mexican film smiles through her tears when she loses the man she loves (*Ebma* 263). In *The Great Ziegfeld*, Luise Rainer stoically conceals from her faithless husband the fact that

---

22 This is also true for Gladys (*BAA*) and for Herminia (*RH*), both of whom do want everything. Herminia dreams of an ordinary, reliable husband but considers seeing the (invented) movie *Lujuria* [Lust], which, she bitterly reflects, would constitute a venture into unknown territory. Manuel Puig once told me that when he thought of the title *Lujuria* he was influenced by *Desiderio* (dir. Roberto Rossellini and Marcello Pagliero, 1943), which was called *El noveno, no desear* [The Ninth, Thou Shalt Not Desire] in Argentina. Herminia embodies the theme of the hopeful spinster, which was frequently found in tangos after 1931 when it was introduced by Enrique Cadícamo. See Ulla, *Tango, rebelión y nostalgia*.

23 Warner, *Alone of All her Sex*, 336, 337.

she is dying (*RH* 76). In *Destino* [Destiny], the mortally wounded Leni bravely assures her lover that they will soon be together again (*Ebma* 100). The "mujer vencida" [broken woman] of the Alfredo LePera epigraph to the tenth instalment of *Boquitas pintadas* restricts herself to a resigned "Es la vida" [That's life] before withdrawing (*Bp* 153). The moribund Marguérite Gautier, played by Garbo in *Camille* (with Robert Taylor, dir. George Cukor, 1936), serenely feigns indifference to Armand (*BAA*, epigraph to chapter 1). Ginger Rogers, in *The Story of Vernon and Irene Castle* (with Fred Astaire, dir. H. C. Potter, 1939), is implausibly courageous when her husband is killed (*RH* 39). Norma Shearer never loses her dignity in *Marie Antoinette* (with Tyrone Power and John Barrymore, dir. W. S. Van Dyke II, 1938), and the stanza from the Homero Manzi tango that precedes the fourth instalment of *Boquitas pintadas* highlights yet another stricken woman who puts a brave face on things (*Bp* 57). Finally, there is the type so often played by the popular Argentine actress Mecha Ortiz, frequently a widow and invariably contained and controlled (*RH* 54, 67; *Bp* 151; *BAA*, epigraph to chapter 12; *Pa* 57).[24]

The need for fundamental spirituality was often emphasized by the clever Hollywood practice of portraying virtuous (that is, asexual), but attractive, women as unwitting victims of their appearance. Molina and his friends, who identify with this condition, refer to themselves as Greta (Garbo), Marilyn (Monroe), Gina (Lollobrigida), and Hedy (Lamarr) (*Ebma* 272), another example of the confusion of actresses and their cinematic roles. It is significant that many of Puig's female creations also identify with, and do their best to imitate, this stereo-

---

24 Mita's friend Choli (*RH*) even tries to look like this actress, and is particularly taken with her (dignified) upswept hairstyle, which presumably contributes to her winning back her husband in the stage version of *The Women* (*RH* 67). The important point for Choli is that Mecha Ortiz was (wrongly) thought to be a widow, and Norma Shearer, who played the same part in the film, actually was. The alternative is indicated by the reference to *Lady Hamilton* (*That Hamilton Woman* in the United States, with Vivien Leigh and Laurence Olivier, dir. Alexander Korda, 1942), in which Emma Hamilton, though never actually married to Nelson, suffers a kind of widowhood and goes under. In *Cae la noche tropical*, Luci and Nidia, both widows, rent a video of this movie, and also of *Waterloo Bridge* (with Vivien Leigh and Robert Taylor, dir. Mervyn Le Roy, 1940), in which the death of her husband obliges Vivien Leigh to sink into prostitution. "Muy tristes" [very sad], they say, not without a certain satisfaction (*Cnt* 45).

type. Choli (*RH*), who finds sex repulsive, constantly experiments with makeup and clothes; Mabel (*Bp*), who is torn between its lure and observing the rules, is in thrall to women's magazines; Gladys (*BAA*), who wants sexual satisfaction and devoted love (as well as a career), is a reader of *Harper's Bazaar*—a North American version of Mabel's *Mundo Femenino*; and Ana (*Pa*), disenchanted with sex though not with love, still adores expensive clothes, perfumes, and accessories. That the stereotype is male-created is clearly indicated in *The Buenos Aires Affair*: when Gladys was a child, her father once suggested that a condition of his approval was her emulation of the girls he admired in the magazine *Rico Tipo*. The last thing he wanted was "una hija loro" [a plain daughter], but it is safe to assume that glamor was not to be equated with loose living (*BAA* 35). All these women are torn between the path of (maternal) virtue demanded by society and the appearance of sexual availability, which seems to be the only way to achieve love.

FEMALE INDEPENDENCE

With two exceptions (Beatriz [*Pa*] and the Young Witch characters alluded to in the cultural references), Puig portrays all women who achieve non-normative control as unhappy and alienated. This stereotype may well be as much a product of male mythology as are other "counterfeited" females, but it is unthinkingly accepted by women who observe traditional paradigms. Clearly, their attitude justifies inertia, or makes their incapacity to change their circumstances more acceptable, but my contention is that the texts reveal the author's fear that *within the system* any break with the patriarchal code may result in loneliness and a sense of failure.

Virtually all his female characters equate emancipation with futility. When Ana (*Pa*) imagines herself as the Actress, she escapes from the prison of marriage only to find herself even more constricted by her profession—and, what is worse, leading a loveless existence. Love has become an "historia que se va! . . . ilusión que se pierde . . . y que nunca volverá . . ." [a story that comes to an end! . . . a lost illusion . . . which will never return . . .] (*Pa* 138). This reflects the fact that Ana herself has made great strides toward liberation: she has divorced a domineering husband, given up her only child, lived alone, had an affair with a married man, earned her own living in a fulfilling way, met influential people, and even made a fresh start with new friends in a foreign country—but she is not happy. Gladys (*BAA*) is another who has ignored the restraints traditionally imposed on women. She is a talented and successful sculptor with half-a-dozen love affairs to her credit in the United States—where women have many more opportunities—but she is neurotic and even suicidal. Mabel and the widow Di Carlo (*Bp*), though not career women, have also shown a certain independence where social strictures are concerned, but it has done them no good. Perhaps the most curious example of this circumstance is Molina (*Ebma*), who has been "a liberated woman," so to speak, all his adult life: he has no experience of the economic and social problems of women, nor has he any idea of what it is like to live with a *macho* man. However, these elements of freedom, which are so obviously desirable, have brought him no comfort.[25]

Cultural allusions mirror this situation and inhibit any desire for change on the part of Puig's female creations. The divorcee in *The Women* (played by Mecha Ortiz on stage and by Norma Shearer in the film with Joan Crawford, Rosalind Russell, Paulette Goddard, and Joan Fontaine, dir. George Cukor, 1939) longs for the love of her ex-husband and finds her mother's views on the benefits of independence unhelpful (*BAA*, epigraph to chapter 7). In fact, the tone of the original Claire Booth Luce play is acerbic, bitchy, and demythifying, but, as with *Mildred Pierce*, Puig consciously chose to emphasize an aspect of it that corresponds to a narrative sub-theme. Another disturbing role model for his characters is the dancer Isadora Duncan, whose film biography, *Isadora* (with Vanessa Redgrave, dir. Karel Reisz, 1968) is referred to by Ana (*Pa* 165). In *Isadora*, the heroine is portrayed as eccentric, bohemian, independent, and self-willed, but never happy. While the much admired Mecha Ortiz in *El canto del cisne* [Swansong] (with Roberto Escalada, dir. Carlos Hugo Christensen, 1945) appears to have learned to live with her enforced independence, she admits that she has achieved this by suppressing her capacity for feeling (*BAA* 185). Emma Hamilton, in *La divina dama*, elected to break all the rules and is spurned by society. Fanny Brice, the real-life heroine of *Funny Girl* (with Barbra Streisand, dir. William Wyler, 1968) is successful in her career but loses her husband, and it may be that it is because this outcome is so self-evident that the conservative María Esther has no wish to see the film (*BAA* 151). A much older movie, which Mabel reads about, depicts a similar situation: *Entre bastidores* (*Stage Door*, with Katherine Hepburn and Ginger Rogers, dir. Gregory La Cava,

---

25 The author's original plan was to make the protagonist of *El beso de la mujer araña* an ultra-conventional woman.

1937) deals with the difficulties faced by young women pursuing a career (*Bp* 140).

Neither passivity nor emancipation is particularly inviting. However, in *The Buenos Aires Affair* we have an encouraging—if not actually misleading—indication that it is possible to have things both ways when Clara Evelia considers the poetry of Alfonsina Storni and Juana de Ibarbourou. Ostensibly, the reference indicates their importance as literary role models who make her feel inferior (*BAA* 28), but it is hard to disregard the difference between the lives of the two women. The Argentine poet Alfonsina Storni[26] always refused to conform: no beauty, she led a hard life as an actress, became an unmarried mother, and ultimately committed suicide. All this may come as no surprise to conservative, conditioned admirers. However, the Uruguayan Juana de Ibarbourou has been described (by Rachel Phillips) as beautiful and feminine and neither coquettish nor sensuous: she found "full satisfaction in being a wife, and wrote charming poems to her husband. When she produced a son, she was an equally contented mother." She was, it seems, as fortunate and blessed as Beatriz (*Pa*), but without the need to be courageous or enterprising. Rachel Phillips claims that she constitutes "an excellent example of the psychology of the oppressed, demonstrating passive acceptance of prevailing circumstances and identification with the oppressor, in this case society at large."[27] However, if the alternative is the type of life led by Alfonsina Storni, as the juxtaposition may well suggest, the situation serves only to confuse Clara Evelia and her contemporaries, for whom, in any case, there is seldom any possibility of choice.

Another ambiguous aspect of female emancipation in Puig's texts that should not be ignored is the danger that emancipation brings to women's relationships with their own sex. Rivalry in love has always existed. As Letty Cottin Pogrebin has observed:

> Men compete for awards and achievements. We compete for men. Men vie for worldly approval and status. We vie for husbands. Men

---

26 She was born in Switzerland, but became an Argentine citizen. See Rachel Phillips, *Alfonsina Storni: From Poetess to Poet* (London: Tamesis, 1975).

27 Phillips, *Alfonsina Storni*, 9.

measure themselves against [their] standards of excellence and an established level of performance. We measure ourselves against each other.[28]

Change will mean that in other spheres, too, women have to face competition from their own sex. This situation is illustrated in Puig's texts by Clara Evelia's resentment at the thought of the superior talent of two women poets (*BAA*), and by the homicidal behavior of the Actress's jealous rival (*Pa*).[29] Perhaps it is not to be wondered at that most women have been content to observe what Dale Spender calls "the male-as-norm" principle for so long.[30] This is manifest in Clara Evelia's complaisant reference to Amado Nervo and Rubén Darío as "maestros" [masters] (*BAA* 28); their superiority does not humiliate her as, she admits, Storni's and Ibarbourou's does.

Ana (*Pa*) is another example of a character who has never been able to relate to other women: she is angry when Pozzi accuses her of this because she cannot deny it. Then, in *Sangre de amor correspondido*, when Maria da Gloria emerges from what may have been a period of insanity caused by the disappearance of the man she loved (but almost certainly was not[31]), she finds that her entry into professional life is impeded by competition from other women (*Sac* 184). Still on a narrative level, in *The Buenos Aires Affair* Gladys's decline as an artist, though inextricably linked with her love for Leo (the male-as-critic), is hastened when the work of another woman (María Esther) is selected to represent Argentina in an international art fair. In the novels, at least, there is little female solidarity: alliances are either emotionally and sexually motivated, like that of the lesbians in *The Buenos Aires*

---

28 Letty Cottin Pogrebin, "Competing with Women," *Ms* 1.2 (1972): 78.

29 Ironically, though she is "una de esas actrices vacuas, que no tienen en la vida más que la carrera" [one of those vacuous actresses who have nothing in their lives but their careers], beauty is still a vital consideration. She is obliged to wear a fine rubber mask to conceal her pockmarked skin (*Pa* 132). In other words, all women are shown as victims of the same values. Hollywood created one of the first outlets for career women, but simultaneously preserved the code by which they were classified according to their looks. In *Pubis angelical*, both women lose: the Actress dies because she is beautiful, but lack of beauty has converted her assassin into "una mujer famosa por su crueldad y determinación" [a woman famous for her cruelty and ruthlessness] (*Pa* 132–33).

30 Spender, *Man Made Language*, 2.

31 See my *The Necessary Dream*, chapter 8.

Affair, or are based on patronage: Beatriz devotes time and energy to defending a servant-girl who has been raped (*Pa* 21). In this context, too, there are no easy solutions.

III

Divided Loyalties

DUTY AND DESIRE

IT IS NOT ONLY women whose impossible choices are elaborated on in Puig's novels. Leo (*BAA*), Larry (*Me*), and Josemar (*Sac*) are the most striking examples of male characters who have to decide between conflicting internal and external pressures, but the same could be said of several others. Not only does men's social supremacy fail to eradicate basic human problems, it often exacerbates them, as Puig himself has said on several occasions. *Machismo* has inflexible rules and values, it is demanding and unforgiving (as Josemar discovers to his cost[1]), and it has its own peculiar difficulties, such as hierarchical considerations, the need to have money in order to preserve an image (a stumbling block for Juan Carlos in *Boquitas pintadas*[2]), and the impossibility of escaping from the egocentric wilfulness that comes from a long history of power consciousness. Even so, Puig's revulsion in the face of these aspects of male-orientated social conditioning never affects his compassion, even toward those who behave reprehensibly.

There are many contexts, both in the narratives and the supporting references, in which heartrending decisions between duty and desire cannot be avoided. Sometimes it is duty to country or family that is in

---

1 See my article *"Sangre de amor correspondido* de Manuel Puig: subjetividad, identidad y paranoia," *Revista Iberoamericana* 155–56 (1991): 469–79.

2 See my study of *Boquitas pintadas* in *Landmarks in Contemporary Latin-American Fiction*, ed. Philip Swanson (London: Routledge, 1990): 207–21.

conflict with the desires of the individual. Traditionally this is a male problem, so that when Ana (*Pa*) begins to be aware of it, it is clear that she has reached a point at which she is determined to behave as if she were a man, rather than conform to the conventional feminine pattern of weakness and irresponsibility. This moment in the text can be located by means of two references that seem arbitrary, but that actually mirror her dilemma (*Pa* 165). The first is to Bellini's *I Puritani* (1835), in which the hero, Arturo, abandons his bride at the altar to flee with another woman; what the distraught heroine does not know is that her apparent rival is the deposed queen, who is being escorted to safety by her bridegroom. He has chosen the path of duty and he is risking his life—for this is England in 1650—as well as his personal happiness.[3]

Patriotism and politics also form the backcloth to Verdi's opera *Nabucco* (1842), which Ana also considers. It tells of Ismaele, a Jew in love with a princess from hostile Assyria who is being held hostage by his people; when he frees her, his fellow countrymen revile him. In the first opera, duty is placed before love; in the second, love before duty. It is more than likely that these allusions are not fortuitous and that they are intended to echo Ana's own situation. However, neither plot will help her to make up her mind. In both cases the lovers are ultimately united and justice reigns, but her two projected scenarios—the stories of the *Ama* and W218—demonstrate her present scepticism on the subject of happy endings. In fact, it is significant that her enjoyment of these operas dates from a past epoch, when a belief in happiness was still possible. Now, as her *Ama* and W218 fictions reveal, she is unconvinced of the efficacy of either of the options open to her.

Toto's choice—if it can be so described—of sexual orientation is also echoed in an operatic correlative: *Il Trovatore* (*RH* 277), which shares with *I Puritani* a scene in which a young man deserts his bride (his duty) for a mother-figure (desire that has not passed into a mature phase). Azucena, the hero's surrogate mother, is to be burnt at the stake, and when he puts her first, it means death both for him and for his beloved. The reference, however indirect, may be an indication of the moment at which the die is cast for the adolescent Toto (*RH* 277). A happy future is unlikely for those who are faced with a situation so

---

3 The title of the opera is echoed when Alejandro is referred to as "a puritan" (*Pa* 100).

impossible that, in practice, any possibility of conscious choice is pre-cluded.

The protagonist of Molina's terrorist film (*Ebma*) also has to choose between his mother and the woman he loves; again it is the mother whose demands are heeded and the younger woman goes away for-ever. Although in general most of the circumstances in the second fic-tion reflect those of Valentín, this particular conflict of interests indicates the situation of his cellmate. The terrorist's mother proves unworthy of his devotion, and this articulation of Molina's growing conviction that filial devotion is no longer the most important factor in his life points to a major change in his outlook. (This time it is loyalty to the mother that may be classified as duty.) It is not long before he decides to dedicate himself to Valentín at the expense of his mother's well-being, claiming that her life is over and that it is now his turn to live (*Ebma* 158). It has been a hard decision to make: *he* is now a terrorist, a "muchacho que abre fuego contra su propia casa" [a young man who sets fire to his own house] (*Ebma* 149).

While this peculiar repudiation of an oedipal complex does not suggest conversion to heterosexuality, Freudian—and Lacanian—theory are still relevant. First of all, Molina is not a homosexual, but a uranist—a woman trapped in a man's body[4]—so that his choice is based on the norms of romantic, heterosexual love. Then, in Lacanian terms, Molina's election of Valentín as a predicate of desire can be judged one of a series of life-giving stimuli, designed to compensate for lack—in this case, explicitly that of the mother.

The heroine of Molina's second film story, *Destino* (a character that may have been suggested by the actress Arletty), is also obliged to choose between desire and patriotism and, once again, the situation closely resembles that of the narrator, Molina. He is male and female while she is both French and German (her first name is French; her last, German). Though she lived as a child in Alsace, "en la frontera, donde a veces ha flameado la bandera alemana" [on the frontier, where the German flag flew from time to time], she was brought up

---

4 The theory of the third sex—men trapped in women's bodies—was proposed by Karl Heinrich Ulrichs (1825–95), author of twelve volumes on homosexuality. It has since been discredited and is not accepted by the vast majority of homo-sexuals, but in its day it had legal implications, since it was assumed that, un-like true homosexuals, uranist subjects had no control whatsoever over their orientation.

to be loyal to France (*Ebma* 60). She has been told to be French, just as Molina has been told to be a man. Little wonder that he claims that if he could choose just one film to see again it would be this one. Although his preference is largely to do with his susceptibility to aesthetics rather than ethics (the film, though beautiful, is full of pro-Nazi propaganda), it also stems from its relevance to his own position.[5] Later, Leni is faced with another impossible choice: just like Molina, she must either become a spy for the enemy or be responsible for the death of an innocent relative.

Audiences are usually sympathetic toward those who have to confront this kind of dilemma, but an ambivalent attitude is inevitable where two of the troubled characters in *Pubis angelical* are concerned. One is Theo, a Russian agent who falls in love with the *Ama* and is torn between loyalty to her and his duty to his masters. The other is his alter ego, LKJS, who deceives W218 in similar fashion. Both of them put commitment and dedication to the cause before love, and the two women in question are ultimately destroyed by this. Since both male characters are fantasized versions of Ana's ex-lover, Pozzi, the nature of her preoccupations and suspicions is illuminated by means of her elaboration of the choice that faces them. The espionage metaphor draws our attention to the fact that each man's initial commitment had been to a form of betrayal, as well as to the unknowable nature of the Other.

In melodrama, the circumstances and the possible consequences of difficult choices are exaggerated for effect. Not infrequently audiences are moved by situations in which a character is only too aware that behavior motivated by altruistic love will be misunderstood and judged dishonorable, wicked, or even criminal, not only by society at large, but also by the person whose best interests are being served. The nightclub singer in Molina's Mexican film (*Ebma* 226 *et seq.*) finds herself in this position when she has to prostitute herself in order to support her seriously ill lover. Another heroine who risks her freedom and her life by fearlessly choosing to trust her love for a man whom she hardly knows is the saintly Minnie in Puccini's *La Fanciulla del West* (1910); Ana talks about this opera to Pozzi (*Pa* 215), who is also an unknown quantity. When he says that he will use the name Ramírez when he returns to Buenos Aires, Ana points out that this is

---

5 The French *Maquis* and the Argentine *montoneros*, both subversive organizations, could never win the support of a bourgeois "woman" like Molina.

the name of the bandit in this opera, but that he is also the romantic hero. She cannot know which Pozzi will turn out to be. When he asks if Ramírez dies, she reveals that the heroine saves him in the nick of time. This allusion once again brings her dilemma into focus.

Later, more is revealed about Pozzi and further parallels with the opera emerge, but by then Ana has refused to lure the *montoneros'* projected victim, Alejandro, to Mexico City and has sent her lover away. The alternative would have been to emulate her operatic counterpart, who was convinced that no one is beyond redemption: indeed, the mysterious Ramerrez (not, in fact, "Ramírez") refers to her pure heart and angelic face (only a cynic would point out that in *lunfardo*, the argot of Buenos Aires, the word *angelito* [angel] means "simpleton"). She could have trusted Pozzi in the same way that Minnie trusted Ramerrez, even after she had discovered his true identity. She could have practiced deception for his sake, as Minnie did by cheating at cards to save Ramerrez's life.[6] In the event she makes the opposite choice; Alejandro survives but, indirectly, her decision causes Pozzi's death.

This is a moment in a Puig text where it is particularly important to be familiar with the background to a passing allusion. From it, we discover that Ana sees herself as innocent and loyal (this is confirmed in her W218 self-projection when she has the treacherous LKJS admit that he admires and respects her [*Pa* 250]), that she is generous (*Pa* 253), and that she considers the possibility of a man being changed by female virtue (*Pa* 255). Whatever Pozzi is *now*, she longs to trust him and to save him, but incipient clearsightedness gives rise to reservations as to the validity of the principles behind the operatic plot. When certain details of the story of Pozzi's journey home come to light, she realizes that he and his motives will always remain a mystery to her: she can interpret the facts as she will. The opera includes a last-minute assertion by the hero that he has never committed murder, only robbery; Pozzi, before he left, swore that he would never become involved in terrorist violence, but Ana learns that this was a lie: he did not enter Argentina by the route he had described (*Pa* 242), and in the final

---

6 Originally a play by David Belasco, the story was filmed in 1930 (with Toto's favorites, Nelson Eddy and Jeanette MacDonald, dir. William Anthony McGuire), and the setting changed to Canada. In this version, the bandit-hero is pursued by the Mounties. In Ana's eyes, the bandits obviously represent the *montoneros*.

shoot-out with the authorities, he had been armed (*Pa* 243). In spite of her good intentions and her soul-searching, she neither changed nor saved Pozzi. Furthermore, any decision regarding her future life and happiness—and his memory—will have to be made without the benefit of knowing the truth behind their relationship.

Even Ana's subsequent concern for the good of her country cannot be judged a traditional happy ending, and our reaction to the intensification of her political consciousness is likely to be as equivocal as it should have been regarding her *volte face* where men are concerned. She may be deluded and she may be misled by others; even if she is not, she may achieve nothing. In the worst possible circumstances, her participation in the political struggle may be counterproductive. In this field, too, the nature of the right choice is impossible to locate. However, even though she once said, "Si en este mundo no te imaginás las cosas lindas estás perdido, porque no existen" [If you don't invent beautiful things in this world, you're finished, because they don't actually exist] (*Pa* 150), she decides to do her duty, in this way—apparently—repudiating fantasy. However, the great adventure of the imagination has not been entirely lost, only transposed into a different key.

THE FLESH AND THE SPIRIT

The flesh and the spirit are frequently in conflict in Puig's narratives, and throughout the texts there are important references to fictional characters and historical figures whose lives have been cursed by imposed choices between these two apparently incompatible areas. Some of these allusions are fleeting and unobtrusive, but none of them, I suggest, is gratuitous.

Massenet's opera *Manon*, which—as we have seen—may illuminate an aspect of Ana's dilemma (*Pa* 165), has a hero who must decide between remaining in a monastery and returning to the mistress who abandoned him for a life of luxury. Despite his awareness that her worldliness has destroyed them both, they are reunited. No good comes of it, however, unless her dying declaration of eternal love can be judged sufficient compensation for his suffering and moral degradation.

Another opera that has already been referred to because of the saintliness of its heroine is Wagner's *Tannhäuser*, but it is the eponymous hero's torment that is relevant in this context. It is particularly so for Herminia (*RH*), who has played part of the work. Tannhäuser's character demonstrates only too clearly that "no se puede tener todo" [you can't have everything],[7] a maxim of which Herminia is unaware as she (like Mabel, in *Boquitas pintadas*) dreams of affection and passion within the same relationship (*RH* 269). The operatic hero's enslavement to Venus, which can be broken only by means of the mediation of the Virgin, points to the utopianism of Herminia's daydreams. Ultimately he is pardoned because Elisabeth gives her life for him (he is saved by the love of a good woman, thereby justifying the unquestioning patient devotion that is a key element in the psychology of the oppressed), but his salvation is not of this world. Therein lies the tragedy of his internal conflict, and of the concomitant pain that is suffered by women who emulate Elisabeth. Carnality and spirituality are portrayed as mutually incompatible, and death is the only solution.

Both *Manon* and *Tannhäuser* are commentaries on the male condition and, in particular, the perceptions of Puig's female creations. In *The Buenos Aires Affair*, however, it is Leo who identifies with an operatic character in an illuminating way (*BAA* 206 *et seq.*) when one of his so-called "sensations" takes the form of an idiosyncratic version of Wagner's *Siegfried* (1876). This is explicitly theatrical; it is a performance that he visualizes, and this authorial device is similar to the inclusion of Molina's equally subjective accounts of films in *El beso de la mujer araña*. In this case, apart from any other consideration, it means that narrative/symbolic variations are acceptable as aspects of a particular production.

While Leo is, so to speak, in the audience of *Siegfried*, the plot of *The Buenos Aires Affair* progresses in clear-cut stages. María Esther, his surrogate mother (as María she is the Virgin; as Esther she is Ishtar to his Hermes), relinquishes her hold on his erect penis and smiles; he strokes her cheek. He puts down his gun, removes the towel that is covering his genitals, and looks over at Gladys. Then he switches on the light so that the three of them are illuminated, as in the climactic moment of the opera. He caresses María Esther, but it is Gladys whom he penetrates. Simultaneously, in his mind's eye he sees the baby Siegfried, who has been born in a cavern and is being brought up by a malevolent dwarf. Next, the baby is a young man, forging the broken sword that will furnish him with power and slaying the dragon that guards the treasure of the Nibelungs. After killing the treacherous

---

7 This is the title of one of the films that Mabel might have seen (*Bp* 140). See chapter II.

dwarf, he penetrates the fiery ring that surrounds the sleeping Brünnhilde and, for the first time, experiences fear. He persists, and the goddess is turned into a mortal by his kiss: "un hombre invencible le ha devuelto la vida" [an invincible man has brought her back to life] (*BAA* 209).

In essence this follows the plot of the opera, but there are one or two modifications and some additions. Most of the changes appear to be unimportant, but we shall return to one that may be significant: in Leo's version, Siegfried kills the dragon by piercing its throat with a sword, whereas in the original legend he stabs it through the heart. The additions are more striking, especially as they serve to make the sexual dimension explicit. First, when both the dragon and the dwarf are dead, the hero takes off his lionskin and stands naked in front of the scandalized audience. Then, when he lifts the warrior's mantle that covers Brünnhilde (in the opera he takes off her armor), he again uncovers himself so that the flames can illuminate their bodies and highlight their differences. Brünnhilde tries to escape, but he kisses and penetrates her. The audience is outraged, but cannot leave as the theatre has inexplicably become a circus marquee without exits. The protagonists fly through the air on a trapeze, looking up to the top of the tent and speculating as to whether it is cold at its pinnacle. The hero, poised on a higher bar, beckons to the heroine to join him so that they can ascend to the heights. Apprehensively, the woman "se lanza al vacío" [leaps into the void] (*BAA* 209)—a favorite Puig phrase. They are now quite alone, there is no safety net, and any slip will mean certain death.

Emphasis on the hero's sexuality suggests a Freudian interpretation of this representation, with Siegfried's natal cavern representing the womb[8] and the malevolent dwarf (*BAA* 206) indicating the phallic dwarf: men are cursed from birth to be phallus bearers—cursed because, as Rupert C. Allen has put it, the phallus "consistently seems to have purposes and desires of his own, whether or not they are in the service of the ego." The dwarf/manikin stands for the "materially creative libido."[9] The treasure guarded by the dragon contains a magic

8 Freud, "Introductory Lectures on Psychoanalysis," *SE* 16 (1916–17).

9 Rupert C. Allen, *Psyche and Symbol in the Theater of Federico García Lorca* (Austin: U of Texas P, 1974) 11.

ring, the usual symbol for the female,[10] and both Freud and Jung associate dragons with father figures. (Leo's other alter ego, Hermes, happens to be the son of Osiris, who is often portrayed as a dragon.[11]) The fact that in *Siegfried* this dragon is a giant in disguise does not invalidate this reading since the giant also represents the father; moreover, in the opera—though Puig makes no mention of this—when Siegfried first appears, he has just slain a bear, yet another paternal symbol.[12] What Puig does emphasize—not inappropriately, given that this is a self-projection of Leo—is the hero's lion skin. Presumably Siegfried was responsible for the death of that animal too (and the lion is also a symbol of the father[13]), but its skin still covers his maleness and impedes his progress, disguising his sexual, and by extension social, identity. The fight with the dragon, an offshoot of ancient fertility rituals, is part of "the development of the hero's masculinity,"[14] and when he acquires power by tasting its spilt blood, he becomes truly male.[15] Now it is clear why he pierces the dragon's throat rather than its heart: the neck is phallic, as well as being the vital area for dismemberment. (Osiris was dismembered, and his cult symbol is the *djed* pillar, representing the head and neck.[16] In Egyptian symbology the phallus and the neck coalesce.) The flames that surround the dormant virgin might be seen as inhibition and anxiety, according to Neumann, who also points out that "with the freeing of the captive and the founding of a new kingdom, the patriarchal age comes into

---

10 In the first opera in the Ring cycle, *Das Rheingold* (1869), Fricka, goddess of marriage, is eager to acquire this ring in order to control her husband, Wotan.

11 Herbert Silberer, *Hidden Symbolism of Alchemy and the Occult Arts*, trans. Smith Ely Jelliffe (New York: Dover, 1971) 200. (Formerly entitled *Problems of Mysticism and its Symbolism*, New York: Moffat, Yard & Co., 1917.)

12 Silberer, *Hidden Symbolism*, 66.

13 C.G. Jung, *Alchemical Studies*, trans. R.F.C. Hull (1967; London: Routledge, 1983) 108, equates the dragon with "the roaring fiery lion." The lion is also popularly associated with another father figure, Saturn. (See Silberer, *Hidden Symbolism*, 128.) The lion could represent youth's undifferentiated stage: in this scenario it is already dead, but what remains of it conceals the hero's masculinity and impedes the acquisition of maturity.

14 Erich Neumann, *The Origins and History of Consciousness*, trans. R.F.C. Hull (1954; London: Routledge, 1973) 198.

15 Silberer, *Hidden Symbolism*, 69.

16 Neumann, *The Origins and History of Consciousness*, 229 *et seq.*

force."[17] It is at this point in the opera that Brünnhilde greets the rising sun, and we remember the solar connotations of Leo's name. The circus coda underlines the danger involved in the couple's newfound independence. Flying, an act associated with the libido in dream analysis, suggests the removal of obstacles.[18] Perhaps the setting also points to the animal, or carnal, nature of the path to the zenith that Leo has taken.

An interpretation based on Section Four (*Der Fall Wagner* [The Case of Wagner]) of Nietzsche's *Die Geburt der Tragödie* [*The Birth of Tragedy*] (1888) is not entirely incompatible with a Freudian reading, but here Siegfried's emancipation must be seen as a revolt against the customs, laws, institutions, and morality of a fossilized society. His battle against morality begins at birth, since he is the product of incest and adultery, and all his actions are designed to eliminate the influence of tradition and respectability and to eradicate fear. His greatest undertaking is to liberate woman, to redeem her via the sacrament of love, and the ensuing twilight of the gods marks the decline of the old system of oppression. However, for all its revolutionary motivation, this theory is reactionary in that it is entirely male-oriented, and there is no breakthrough for either sex: the passive woman is not protected from danger, and impossible demands are made of the dominant man.

Yet another reading of this section of the novel is possible with recourse to the theories of Jung. Symbolic "immaterial values" can be attached to Jung's "treasure hard to attain," according to Neumann, and the captive really represents "something within—namely the soul herself." The dragon is therefore the Terrible Mother, and its destruction will mark "the formation of the higher ego," after which "the victorious hero stands for a new beginning, the beginning of creation." The dragon, like the malevolent dwarf, may indicate "the dangers of the unconscious."[19] This, then, is a quest for *spiritual* treasure; Jung claims that the dragon's defeat leads to "entrance into the head [the

---

17 Neumann, *The Origins and History of Consciousness*, 201, 199.

18 Silberer, *Hidden Symbolism*, 86.

19 Neumann, *The Origins and History of Consciousness*, 195, 196, 123, 124–25.

temple, since the dragon so often guards the door of the temple[20]], and the way to conscious knowledge and understanding." Then the sun truly rises.[21] The mortal blow to the breast, rather than the throat, would have much more significance in this interpretation, with the nourishment provided by the magic blood recalling the legend of the pelican, which Honorius of Autun saw as symbolizing Christ.[22] The concept of maturity is very different here. However, this theory fails to cover the element of sexual union with Brünnhilde, and casts no light on Puig's additions to the original story, particularly the circus coda. Leo's projected apotheosis is not, I would suggest, spiritual, and it is this that is dangerous. As Jung himself once said, "the blinder love is, the more it is instinctual, and the more it is attended by destructive consequences, for it is a dynamism that needs form and distinction."[23]

However repellent some aspects of Leo's behavior may be, it would be unjust to claim that he has *chosen* the way of the flesh. He is a victim of its demands, and these are exacerbated by social conditioning; as a result he is both neurotic and (sporadically) remorseful. Leo represents an extreme condition, for his masculinity is his most important characteristic, a fact that is symbolized by his disproportionately large genitals, his obsession with sex, and repeated references to his lack of control (many of his actions are accompanied by phrases such as "como si alguien le hablase al oído" [as if someone else were speaking in his ear]) (*BAA* 92, 100, etc.). His inability to achieve sexual satisfaction could hardly be seen as his fault.

The "sensation" that precedes Leo's vision of Siegfried represents another moment in his continuing struggle. This time his model is St. Sebastian, who combines spirituality with potency, but, as in the case of Tannhäuser, this leads to a tragic outcome. Leo thinks of this saint

---

20 Marcellin Berthelot, in *Les Origines d'alchimie* (Paris, 1895) 60, quotes the following from an old manuscript: "The dragon is the guardian of the temple. Sacrifice it, flay it, separate the flesh from the bones, and you will find what you seek."

21 Jung, *Alchemical Studies*, 89.

22 Honorius of Autun, "Speculum de mysteriis ecclesias," in *Patrologiae cursus completus*, ed. Jacques Paul Migne, 221 vols. (Paris, 1844–64), Latin Series, 172, cols. 807–1108.

23 Jung, *Alchemical Studies*, 297. Although Jung is talking about Christian love, his judgment is appropriate here.

when he realizes that both Gladys and María Esther are looking at his genitals. María Esther takes hold of his penis and jokingly asks: "¿Qué tenés acá? ¿un pajarito?" [What have we here? A little birdie?] (*BAA* 204), echoing a game that his sister Olga (another surrogate mother) had played with him when he was a child (*BAA* 93). It is at this moment that he conjures up the Praxiteles statue of Hermes in his mind's eye, and then, as he becomes conscious of a gradual erection, his thoughts turn to Michaelangelo's "Last Judgment." (It is surely not fortuitous that the section begins: "el papa Sixto IV erigió una capilla en el Vaticano . . ." [Pope Sixtus IV *erected* a chapel in the Vatican . . .], *BAA* 205; emphasis added.) In the painting, the robust and manly figure of St. Sebastian, who is clutching a sheaf of arrows in hands that suggest "fuerza y decisión" [strength and decisiveness], is distinguished by unusually large genitals. Like Leo himself, as well as the sexually mature baby he imagined in a previous "sensation," Sebastian is strikingly male, but his face is gentle and sensitive, his curly hair is long, and he gives the impression of kindliness and beauty. Even the coloring of the figure is monochromatic, unlike that of all the others. His vital energy has been channelled into spirituality, and he dies. As Walter Pater once said, "in Michaelangelo, people have for the most part been attracted or repelled by the strength, while few have understood his sweetness."[24] The equivocal, if not sinister, implications of sweetness are only too evident to Leo.

Another Puig character preoccupied by the conflict between body and soul is Larry (*Me*). His situation is somewhat different, for several reasons. First, he is an intellectual and has studied philosophy and politics, as well as psychoanalysis. Second, his maleness is less oppressive than Leo's. Finally, he was once influenced by a religious education, something that cannot be said of any of the other protagonists of Puig's novels (apart from Teté [*RH*]), and he has experienced a period of faith. Nevertheless, he does not understand himself, even if he thinks he does. Furthermore, he is not in sympathy with other people, he has completely abandoned sexual activity, and he now regards his shortlived devotion to the Church as an adolescent phase during

---

24 Walter Pater, "The Poetry of Michaelangelo," in his *The Renaissance: Studies in Art and Poetry* (1873; London: Collins, 1961) 85. Pater asserts that Michaelangelo portrayed "the austere truths of human nature" (88), which might help to account for the inclusion of such an important reference to the figure of St. Sebastian within the narrative.

which religion provided an outlet for nascent sexual energy. His study of the Bible and the Prayer Book does not appear to have helped him any more than his fascination with the writings of St. Augustine (*Me* 143, 144), though in the latter he might well have found a model, since this saint agonized at length before choosing God instead of honors, wealth, and marriage, and was ordained against his will. Understandably, Larry finds it impossible to reconcile his knowledge of the world and the flesh with the divine nature. Even his liking for religious pictures—"esas pinturas medioevales voluptuosas . . . en que María amamanta a Jesús" [those voluptuous medieval paintings . . . in which Mary is nursing Jesus]—is directed toward the human, maternal aspect of the Virgin, with her "sonrisa de satisfacción" [satisfied smile] (*Me* 148–49). It is not all that strange that he should focus on this since, as Marina Warner has observed, only one "natural biological function . . . was permitted the Virgin in Christian cult—suckling,"[25] and the *Maria Lactans* image was once common. On the other hand, since the nursing Madonna disappeared from Marian iconography about four hundred years ago, the reference emphasizes the extent of Larry's preoccupation with what it represents.

The flesh/spirit dichotomy is often indicated with great subtlety. When, for example, Héctor refuses to read "los libracos de Echeverría" [Echeverría's great tomes] (*RH* 162), it may be that, in addition to signalling his philistine reaction to anything thought of as High Art, the reference is inviting the reader to consider the author. Echeverría's importance for Argentina will be dealt with in another section, but for the moment it may be helpful to remember his insistence on the civilization/barbarism dichotomy, illustrated by the bestial Indian men and the pure, noble protagonists of his well-known narrative poem *La cautiva* [The Captive Woman] (1837), which highlights the dual nature of men.

There is a connection between *La cautiva* and "los tangos a la Valentino" that are being played when the *Ama* meets Theo for the first time (*Pa* 44). The original link—that Rudolph Valentino, in his most famous film, *The Sheik* (with Agnes Ayres, dir. George Melford, 1921), captures an English girl, the counterpart of Echeverría's *cautiva*—is a tenuous one, but it is often by means of these hazy, possibly subconscious, connections that deep communication between author and reader is made possible. In both tales, spiritual values are

---

25 Warner, *Alone of All Her Sex*, 192. In fact, the Virgin also weeps.

admired and shown as paramount. María in *La cautiva* is as sublimely immaculate as her name suggests, while the heroine of the Valentino film selflessly nurses her sick captor back to health, simultaneously reducing his aggressive maleness to a level of compromise domesticity. It comes as no surprise to hear that Héctor, who personifies uncouth *machismo*, finds nothing to relate to in Echeverría; conversely, the *Ama* (*Pa*), an oppressed woman, cannot fail to be consoled by the sexually ambiguous figure of Valentino and the tangos that bring him to mind. That her lover, Theo, is also Thea is compatible with the theme of sexual ambiguity.

This is not the only occasion on which Puig mentions Rudolph Valentino, and these references may be seen as connected to the novelist's concern with sexual identity. Though almost always embodying frightening and irresistible male passion on the screen, Valentino was frequently cut down to size by a woman—either by a *femme fatale* (in the silent version of *Blood and Sand* [with Nita Naldi, dir. Fred Niblo, 1922]), by a good-bad woman, or by an innocent virgin.[26] In real life, the actor was accused of being homosexual, and he often aroused male hostility; he has also been called androgynous, as well as being classified as "an icon for lovelorn ladies and for homosexuals alike."[27] All of this mirrors Puig's view of the universal capacity for bisexual behavior—and, indeed, its desirablity—which is evident in both the main text and the footnotes of *El beso de la mujer araña*: even the name Molina is "la féminisation du nom commun 'molino'" [a feminine version of the common noun "molino"][28] but to call a man who is apparently the antithesis of all that Molina stands for "Valentín" suggests not only *valentía* [courage], *valiente* [brave]—and, of course, St. Valentine—but also Rudolph Valentino.[29] Molina's femininity is underlined every time his name is mentioned, for his (unequivocally masculine) Christian names, Luis Alberto, are used only in official reports. On the other hand, Valentín reacts angrily when any reference

---

26 Fear of emasculation is one basis for the male response to the *femme fatale* figure, who is judged the incarnation of the Archetypal Feminine.

27 David Thomson, *A Biographical Dictionary of the Cinema* (London: Secker & Warburg, 1975) 575.

28 Milagros Ezquerro, *Que raconter c'est apprendre à mourir: Essai d'analyse de "El beso de la mujer araña" de Manuel Puig* (Toulouse: U of Toulouse-Le Mirail; Institut d'Études Hispaniques et Hispano-Américaines, 1981) 40.

29 Ezquerro, *Que raconter c'est apprendre à mourir*, 48.

is made to his feminine characteristics: when his cellmate calls him "niña Valentina" [Miss Valentina], he replies: "No me llames Valentina, que no soy mujer" [Stop calling me Valentina; I'm not a woman] (*Ebma* 43, 44). Puig was well aware that Rudolph Valentino's real name was actually Valentina.

Another instance of the struggle between body and soul is hinted at when the Actress (*Pa*) insists on calling her last lover "Él" [He]. It suggests a messianic role, but it could also bring the well-known Buñuel film to mind: the hero of *Él* (with Arturo de Córdova, 1952) is another who is torn between a religious education and his sexual urges and experience. Then there is the poet Amado Nervo, so admired by Clara Evelia (*BAA* 28), who is said to have suffered from the incompatibility between "un ansia religiosa" [religious longings] and "los deseos de la carne" [desires of the flesh].[30] Perhaps the most revealing of all the examples is an invented tale that Toto claims is by Chekhov (*RH* 276).[31] The crux of the story is the indifference of a would-be seducer once he is in a position to achieve his aim. "Quiere y no quiere, siente y no siente" [He wants to, and yet he doesn't; he feels, and yet he doesn't], says René Alberto Campos, for whom this duality reflects Toto's sexual ambivalence: "el otro, como objeto del deseo, no es del otro sexo, sino el cuerpo masculino [that of his schoolmate Adhemar] [o] su propio cuerpo" [the Other, as the object of desire, does not belong to the opposite sex, but has a male body (or it is) his own body]. It might also be alleged that the character's ambivalence reflects a reluctance to accept the flesh in any form whatsoever.

Toto is a sensitive, effeminate child, but "real men" are unlikely to emulate those who have unequivocally chosen the spirit and denied the flesh, such as St. Francis, who is mentioned by the religiously inclined Teté (*RH* 108): when leaving on business trips, her father says that he will disguise himself as St. Francis so that God will think him virtuous. "No lo dice en serio" [He's joking], explains the naïve young

---

30 Andrew Debicki, *Antología de la poesía mexicana moderna* (London: Tamesis, 1977) 53.

31 This has been dealt with in an illuminating way by René Alberto Campos (*Espejos*, 106–07), who relates this moment in Toto's life to his isolated enjoyment of *Cuéntame tu vida* (*Spellbound*, with Ingrid Bergman and Gregory Peck, dir. Alfred Hitchcock, 1954), in which an amnesiac hero does not know if he is guilty of murder.

girl. That he should say it at all gives us some idea of the real nature of his extra-mural activities. In this context, it is hardly surprising either that Dostoyevsky, who placed so much emphasis on spiritual values, should be another of the *macho* Héctor's *bêtes noires* (*RH* 159). The ascetic life is hard and it may even be undesirable, but the examples of those who ignore it are frightening indeed. Men turn into wolves as in *El hombre lobo* (*The Wolf Man*),[32] or blood-sucking vampires like Dracula, and women become voracious wild animals: this is best exemplified by the unhappy heroine of *Cat People* and her prototype in the legend set in the days of the Crusades (*Ebma* 18).

Many of the Hollywood actors who are favorites with Puig's female characters constitute misleading examples of the longed-for happy medium between spirituality/beauty and carnality. On another plane, Gladys finds a similar model in one of her best-loved authors, Hermann Hesse (*BAA* 33, 46). *Demian* (1919), a favorite book, seems to prove that compromise is possible. Its confused and neurotic hero, Sinclair, is persuaded by his friend Demian to be less moralistic, to break free from his parents' pietism, and to face up to the fact that sexuality and self-assertion are not necessarily evil. The satisfying happy ending of this *Bildungsroman* may have contributed toward Gladys's determination to pursue the twin aims of romantic—that is, spiritual—love and sensual gratification, but she is defeated by reality.

The texts suggest that, traditionally, men judge themselves diminished by any form of compromise where conditioned sexual norms are concerned. The power they see as their right is very fragile. The debate as to why this should be so began with the birth of psychoanalysis, but even today no one is sure if it is true that "the castration threat is . . . an embodiment of a cultural imperative which continues to enforce its demands on the mind through the structures of the superego," neither is there any way of knowing if it is this that "shatters the Oedipus complex and hence forces the acquisition of a sexed identity"[33] that then has to be preserved at all costs. Can it be that since "the transition from one sexual 'stage' to another is achieved and necessitated through

---

32 There may also be some connection with the fact that Juan Domingo Perón was born in Lobos. Puig's ingenuity should not be underestimated.

33 Jeffrey Weeks discusses Freud's later theories in these terms in *Sexuality and its Discontents: Meanings, Myths and Modern Sexualities* (London: Routledge, 1985) 141.

deprivation,"[34] any modification of the state that has been reached must be accompanied by dread? Or is it predominantly a social problem, with the power acquired in a phallocentric society represented by potency on a biological level? Is the desire for supremacy based on an assumption that we know ourselves by being sure about our sexual identity? The fundamental question is whether "the fear of castration [is] so significant because the penis is naturally the superior organ, or [if it is] because of its symbolic importance in a male-dominated culture."[35] Puig obliges his readers to examine, if not challenge, the view that clear-cut sexual differentiation is essential to social order, but his writings also reflect the Freudian claim that the fear of death is closely related to the fear of castration.[36] He does not furnish dogmatic answers; he merely indicates important (and possibly unanswerable) questions in the narratives and underlines their presence by means of cultural references.

The most explicit example of male reduction is found in *Maldición eterna a quien lea estas páginas* (157–58) when Larry, talking about his most profound fears, tells Ramírez the story of the film *The Incredible Shrinking Man* (with Grant Williams, dir. Jack Arnold, 1957).[37] In this film, a man who finds himself in the middle of a radioactive fog becomes smaller and smaller. In Larry's version, emphasis is placed on the hero's relationship with his wife: "al lado de la esposa se ve más bajo" [he gets smaller and smaller compared with his wife]. Then, even though she is "muy comprensiva en todo momento, y constantemente le da prueba de su cariño, . . . se irrita por todo *y se desquita con ella*" [invariably very understanding and constantly providing proof of her love, . . . everything infuriates him *and he takes it out on her*] (emphasis added). Larry adds: "Es como si le arrebatasen la masculinidad, porque la esposa está siempre presente cada vez que algo lo humilla" [It's as though his maleness were being taken away from him, because his wife is present every time he is humiliated]. Later, when Ramírez thinks that Larry has something urgent to tell him, he imagines the

---

34 Juliet Mitchell, *Psychoanalysis and Feminism* (1974; Harmondsworth: Penguin, 1982) 26.

35 Weeks, *Sexuality and its Discontents*, 141.

36 Freud, "The Ego and the Id," *SE* 19 (1923).

37 Puig originally planned an allusion to *The Incredible Hulk* (1977), a television film directed by Kenneth Johnson.

younger man saying that he is in terrible danger and surrounded by total darkness (*Me* 188)—perhaps the equivalent of the radioactive fog of the movie. When he finally persuades Larry to reveal the secrets of his marriage, we discover that he blames its breakdown on his wife's humiliating behavior. In her disenchantment she had begun to drink heavily, and it was not long before their lovemaking turned into "un acto de odio" [an act of hatred] (*Me* 244). Fear, once again, became loathing. He explains her infidelity by claiming that she had expected too much from him: "algo muy especial" [something extraordinary] (*Me* 246).[38]

Mention of Icarus in *The Buenos Aires Affair* again draws the reader's attention to this problem. At an early stage in her life, Gladys's male rival in a sculpture competition creates a "gigantic" statue of this symbol of overweening ambition, whose downfall was brought about by his flying too near the sun, with its connotations of masculine potency and force (*BAA* 37). In fact, it is Gladys who wins the competition: the female has defeated the male. That might have been the end of the story, but the young sculptor makes another appearance much later in the text and we learn that Gladys's early success had been a Pyrrhic victory: her present unhappiness is not the result of professional or artistic problems, but is caused by sexual and emotional frustration. In a moment of anguish, she tries to recall the features of her erstwhile rival, and she indulges in an unsatisfying act of masturbation as she does so (*BAA* 232). Because of her conditioning, she cannot believe that any good can come of professional equality between the sexes and she is convinced that her earlier triumph has inhibited her relationships with men. The author's equivocal position is manifest in the many narrative indications that this view may be an accurate one.

AESTHETICS VERSUS ETHICS

The reader's reaction to the film *Destino* [Destiny], recounted by Molina in *El beso de la mujer araña*, will surely coincide with that of Valentín, who classifies it as an "inmundicia nazi" [a piece of Nazi

---

38 The title *The Incredible Shrinking Man* also suggests the slang term "shrinks" for psychoanalysts. The original version of this novel was written in English; when Puig translated it into Spanish, he used the (non-existent) Spanish term *reductores de cabezas* [headshrinkers].

filth] (*Ebma* 63). In view of the prevalence of pro-German feeling in Argentina during the Second World War, he could reasonably assume that Molina had shared in this, but we discover that in fact there is no ideological basis for the older man's fond memories of the film. He knows perfectly well that "los maquis . . . eran los patriotas" [the *Maquis* . . . were the patriots] (*Ebma* 85), and when his cellmate asks him if he realizes that they were "verdaderos héroes" [true heroes], his answer is angrily dismissive: "Che, pero me creés más bruta de lo que soy" [What do you take me for, man? An even stupider woman than I am?] (*Ebma* 98). What makes this movie important for him is that it is full of "cosas lindas" [beautiful things], and Molina is not to be persuaded by Valentín's argument that thinking about such things can be dangerous (*Ebma* 85). Perhaps there is something to be said for Molina's outlook; certainly it is not long before Valentín, too, shows undisguised interest in what happens to the fictional protagonists, despite his previous resistance. "No me gusta, pero estoy intrigado" [I don't like it, but I'm intrigued], he confesses (*Ebma* 85).

Once again, loyalties are divided. If, as Puig himself has argued, beauty has little to do with socially dictated quality in art, neither can it be said to be confined to works that are morally or ideologically respectable. Conversely, much bad art contains worthy ethical or ideological premises. Is there really any danger in enjoying the aesthetic at the expense of the moral, as Valentín suggests? If there is, how does this relate to other themes that have become apparent in Puig's novels?

The view that "good" equals highbrow is, of course, marginally more defensible than delight in art that is ethically repugnant. Even so, Leslie Fiedler's views on the latter circumstance are very convincing. While he admits that it would be a mistake

> simply to stand the traditional rank order on its head by insisting that what pleases the many should be judged "good" and therefore be preserved, perhaps even taught, while that which is available only to the few, and therefore divides class from class, should be condemned, perhaps even banned,

he argues that we should create "an approach to literature in which we will, if not quite abandon, at least drastically *downgrade both ethics and*

aesthetics in favour of ecstatics" (emphasis added).[39] Aesthetic appeal
is so much more potent than any ethical infrastructure, and the dichotomy is particularly in evidence in Puig's novels, since there are so
many allusions to popular taste, which is especially immune to ideology.[40] Because of its visual impact, this is probably more true of the
cinema than of any other genre. The pro-Nazi film is but one example
of an ideologically unacceptable product that is both visually attractive
and emotionally appealing: the German soldiers are all "rubios, bien
lindos" [fair and terribly handsome] (*Ebma* 55), the heroine, Leni, is
"una mujer divina, alta, perfecta" [a divine, tall, perfect woman] (57),
the hero's apartment is "lujosísimo" [the height of luxury] (61), and
love is depicted as tragically overwhelming. It is easy to understand
the attraction of all this for Molina. As Fiedler has remarked, we are
moved "viscerally rather than cerebrally, at a level where 'both/and'
displaces 'either/or', and we can have our cake and eat it too." For
example, "we find it possible . . . to respond passionately to the
triumphs of Tarzan and the sufferings of Scarlett O'Hara, even as we
are being repelled by their authors' politics," and he concludes that
"there is something profoundly disturbing about the power of vulgar
works . . . to move us at a level beneath that of our conscious alleg-
iances, religious or political."[41] It is a short step from this argument
to the confusion of female beauty with virtue, which almost invariably
results in disillusion. Puig links these two forms of (self-) deception in
the character of Toto, who is disoriented by the discovery that even a
lovely woman "hace traiciones" [betrays you] (*RH* 82), and in Molina
(in many ways an adult version of Toto), who consciously ignores his
better judgment.

Mass culture may be particularly immune to moral strictures, but
it could also be claimed that much highbrow art has little to do with
ethics; furthermore, the presence and quality of culture in a given
society bears no relation to its standards of morality. Both these truths
are pinpointed repeatedly in the novels. When Leo is being tortured
(*BAA* 103), his aggressors have the radio switched on, and the scene

---

39 Leslie Fiedler, *What Was Literature? Class Culture and Mass Society* (1982; New
   York: Simon, 1984) 128, 139.

40 Fiedler, *What Was Literature?*, 197.

41 Fiedler, *What Was Literature?*, 133, 195. An example is Alfred Hitchcock's observation that in any film in which an burglar is about to be surprised *in flagrante*
   by the householder, the audience's sympathies will always be with the intruder.

is played out in a thought-provoking atmosphere of cruelty and cheerful songs, reminiscent of the orchestras that played outside Nazi gaschambers. Héctor, who embodies crass animality and insensitivity, is taken with Tchaikovsky and Beethoven (*RH* 170); Leo (though—significantly—he denies it at first) used to sing "Lilli Marlene," a sentimental song about eternal fidelity, with his sister (*BAA* 137–38); and in what is perhaps the most famous and aesthetically pleasing scene in *The Great Waltz*, the sweet song of the birds in the Vienna Woods inspires Johann Strauss to write charming music at the very moment when his adulterous relationship with Carla begins. Even Leo's likening his own childhood appearance to that of Toulouse-Lautrec (*BAA* 138) suggests the gulf between beauty and reality, for, as Werner Haftmann has observed, in this painter's conception of life "the 'beautiful' was divorced from the 'good' and the 'true'."[42]

The dichotomy between culture and social morality is made explicit in *Pubis angelical*, and the protagonists' puzzlement is not surprising if we are aware of the universality of the immature belief in the link between aesthetic beauty and virtue. That it is indeed immature is confirmed by the age at which Toto wakes up to Rita Hayworth's true motives in the film *Blood and Sand*. In Puig's later novel, Ana and Pozzi recall the great variety of operas, concerts, and films in Buenos Aires in 1972 (*Pa* 165–66), and Pozzi adds: "En pleno gobierno militar, qué contradicción" [at the height of the military régime, what a contradiction].[43] The right-wing Peronist Alejandro is the embodiment of this: Ana finds him hateful and sinister (*Pa* 35, 37), and he is ruthlessly single-minded and even demonic if Pozzi's nickname for him— Beelzebub—is anything to go by (*Pa* 99). Yet at the same time he is undeniably cultured and he adores music (*Pa* 232). It is difficult to ignore the parallel with Hitler's passion for Wagner.[44]

---

42 Werner Haftmann, *Painting in the Twentieth Century*, 2 vols. (1961; London: Lund Humphries, 1965) 1: 47.

43 This was when General Alejandro A. Lanusse was in power. Although he promised elections to restore civil government, military rule persisted for two years (1971–73), a period distinguished by the struggle between the armed services and guerilla groups, as well as by torture and violence.

44 According to Joachim C. Fest, *Hitler*, trans. Richard and Clara Winston (1973; Harmondsworth: Penguin, 1977) 37, the young Hitler "succumbed to the music of Richard Wagner and often went to the opera night after night," and it is well known that his favourite opera was *Die Meistersinger*. The parallel with Hitler

The image of blindness is frequently found in Puig's novels, and its implications are many. Among these is that the sightless will not be misled by what is only superficial—particularly beauty. For example, the blind narrator of *The Enchanted Cottage* (*Ebma*), like Marianela's Pablo, is able to discern the real worth of a woman because he is not distracted by plain features. Where the arts are concerned, the converse is often the case: audiences enjoy sensorial and emotional gratification and turn a blind eye to suspect values. One aspect of the danger referred to by Valentín is collective susceptibility to insidious manipulation, but it could also be argued that a preference for the aesthetic may harm the individual psyche. This is a problem for Ana (*Pa*) as well as for Molina. She realizes that a taste for *espectáculos* (that is, for being a spectator who unthinkingly emulates the behavior of others) entails, like her preferred setting for lovemaking, the element of darkness (*Pa* 192), and this, of course, is tantamount to the wrong sort of blindness. In both situations conditioned utopianism alienates the subject from reality. As Valentín says, "te podés volver loco . . . alienándote" [you can go crazy . . . and become alienated] (*Ebma* 85), suggesting that on a personal level self-deception is as pernicious as collective misguidedness. These come together in Ana, whose own future is inextricably linked to that of society, whether she wishes this or not, and her dilemma is encapsulated in an operatic reference. After claiming that an ideal world would be full of feminine sensibility, she goes on to allude to Mozart's opera *Così fan tutte* (1790), a reference that makes a vital difference to the reading of this passage. For her,

> un mundo hecho por mujeres tendría que ser como un dúo de Fiordiligi y Dorabella en *Così fan tutte*, un mundo donde todo es gracia, soltura, liviandad. . . . un mundo armonioso, al que se haya venido para gozar cada minuto de nuestra existencia. *Si los hombres tuviesen más música adentro del corazón, . . . el mundo sería diferente.* Pero todo lo lindo nos lo acaparamos nosotras, a ellos les tocó todo lo feo
> . . .

---

is underlined in Ana's claim that in the Teatro Colón, the *porteños* heard Wagner "cantado por elencos dignos de Bayreuth" [sung by casts worthy of Bayreuth] (*Pa* 192). In later years, Hitler is reported to have remarked to a boyhood friend that "it all began" in Bayreuth after an inspiring performance of *Rienzi*. Fest takes this anecdote from August Kubizek, *Adolf Hitler, mein Jugenfreund* (Graz and Göttingen: L. Stocker, 1953).

[a world created by women would be like a duet by Fiordiligi and Dorabella in *Così fan tutte,* a world where everything is graceful, easy and light . . . a world full of harmony, where the aim would be to enjoy every moment of existence. *If men had more music in their hearts, . . . the world would be different.* But we women have kept all that for ourselves, they've finished up with everything that's ugly . . .] (*Pa* 231–32; emphasis added).

However, her simplistic shortsightedness is underlined by the plot of the opera in which the two sisters indulge in calculated deception of their respective suitors. Order is restored only when everyone realizes that illusions are worthless: life has to be lived as it is and people recognized for what they are. So it is that Puig indirectly reveals that Ana's manichaean gender classification is no more accurate than were her earlier assumptions about male superiority. The beautiful music is a red herring.

On a socio-political level, the message is even more obvious, as the effect of the pro-Nazi film on Molina demonstrates. Valentín's view is that he must look beyond what is immediately visible; if he does not, he is a fool, and an immoral fool at that. Yet Ana is right when she claims that what is harsh and ugly offers no pleasure or consolation. Molina is convinced that complete alienation would result from facing up to things as they are, and for many years Ana shared this view: "Sin esa ilusión no me importa vivir un minuto más" [Without that dream I have no interest in going on living], she once admitted (*Pa* 193). It is not a question of whether a change of outlook is possible, for Ana's story proves that it is, but of whether the human psyche can, or should, be persuaded that it is totally desirable.

KNOWLEDGE AND EMOTION

Of all the novels, it is *Maldición eterna a quien lea estas páginas* that best illustrates Puig's perception of the incompatibility between knowledge and emotion, both in the narrative and by means of a relatively large number of supporting references to works of art and philosophy. This text contains indications that the author saw the emotional life as vital to the pursuit of happiness, even when it is in conflict with rationality: human beings are nourished by desires, faith, imagination, and even fantasizing, however indefensible this may be in the cold light of day. Both protagonists illustrate this point of view, but Larry's background and attitudes are given more detailed attention than those of Ramírez.

When Larry first meets the old Argentine exile, his life is empty and static: empty because he is divorced, estranged from his family, and living on his own; static because he has no job and no sense of direction. His only objective is to earn enough to survive, and he is deeply unhappy.

Initially, the cat-and-mouse game that the two men play with each other seems to be entirely based on the older man's search for knowledge. It is not long, however, before we discover that it is knowledge of how to *feel* that the amnesiac Ramírez needs to re-acquire, and that, in fact, both men share the same predicament. Furthermore, Larry's emotional deprivation might be judged even more tragic than that of Ramírez because of his comparative youth: he, at least, still has time to live. The irony of his situation is plain. He is a man who has had the benefit of all the standard forms of consolation for human unease. As a boy he was fervently religious. Then he dedicated himself to the comprehension of society—eschewing liberal humanist individualism— by means of the study of politics and philosophy, and he found what seemed a complete answer in Marxism. Finally, he combined concern for himself and for the community by becoming involved in psychoanalysis. When the text begins, he is undeniably knowledgeable and, compared with Puig's other characters, well educated, but it is all to no avail, for he is neither content nor balanced. Eventually he does feel the desire to start living again, but now his ambitions are no longer utopian: his rejection of teaching as a profession means that he is refusing to pontificate, and indicates his realization that there is no body of facts that can furnish a definitive solution to human problems. Vaguely understood and wrongly applied information, theories, and generalizations may actually be counterproductive. The title of this novel can be explained in these terms (as well as in others), for the "eternal curse" awaits those who think that knowledge constitutes the road to personal fulfillment. In fact, its consequences can be despair and evil, for human beings are intellectually as well as morally imperfect, and in any case, as Aldous Huxley once said, "the history of ideas is to a great extent the history of the misinterpretation of ideas."[45]

In the contemporary world the problem is complicated by the realization that the search for knowledge is not just a question of account-

---

45 Aldous Huxley, *Ends and Means: An Enquiry into the Nature of Ideals and into the Methods Employed for their Realization* (London: Chatto & Windus, 1938) 227.

ing for everything in physical terms, or by means of scientific material-ism: if we are aware of Jung's "spirit of the age," we know that modern humanity has discarded both of these approaches.[46] In modern times the quest for knowledge is an eminently respectable pro-cess, for it is undertaken in fields such as philosophy and psychology, neither of which disregards emotions and feelings, and, perhaps for the first time in history, it is based on the hope that "Know thyself" may not be an impossible injunction. However, "knowledge," as cur-rently defined, can be just as easily misinterpreted as scientific facts; it is viewed by some in a fashion so utopian that it rivals the illusions of previous generations in its inefficacy. Even psychoanalysis is con-verted into ideology by some—that is, into "a system of thought which claims to be total,"[47] one that is "accomplished by the so-called thinker consciously . . . but with a false consciousness."[48] Larry, whose self-image has actually been deformed by psychoanalysis, is a fictional example of this.

Psychologists argue that there is a difference between feelings and emotion, but in this novel the two concepts may be said to come to the same thing: "Emotion-therapy really means dealing with something other than emotion," according to James Hillman, "attitude, physiol-ogy, instincts, etc.," because "emotion is . . . an accompanying epiphenomenon."[49] It is also worth bearing in mind the theory that representations result from emotion: Plotinus, for example, held that emotions could arise independently of ideas.[50] Moreover, in modern times it has been asserted that emotion can control memory, and this may be what has happened to Ramírez: if he really has forgotten the past, his sense of guilt could be the cause. It should not be forgotten, either, that emotion provides the ground for images (the imagination) as well as thought; evaluations of the results of psychosurgery have shown that any diminution of emotional tension goes hand in hand

---

46 C.G. Jung, *Modern Man in Search of a Soul* (1953; London: Routledge, 1962), es-pecially chapter 9: "The Basic Postulates of Analytical Psychology."

47 Janine Chasseguet-Smirgel and Béla Grunberger, *Freud or Reich? Psychoanalysis and Illusion*, trans. Claire Pajaczkowska (New Haven: Yale UP, 1986) 15.

48 F. Engels, "Letter to Franz Mehring, 14 July 1893," in *Marx and Engels: Basic Writings on Politics and Philosophy*, ed. L. Feuer (London: Fontana, 1969) 446.

49 James Hillman, *Emotion: A Comprehensive Phenomenology of Theories and their Meanings for Therapy* (London: Routledge, 1960) 47.

50 Plotinus, *Enneads* III.6.4.

with impoverishment of the imagination, as well as reduced creativity in the fields of art, literature, music, and theatre.[51]

Both Larry and Ramírez have repressed their emotions, and with them the life-enhancing elements of their existence. Larry has substituted knowing for feeling, while Ramírez has taken refuge in amnesia. However, as the older man's irresistible passion to rejoin life demonstrates, he finds this intolerable. It is not without interest that one of the most frequently mentioned aspects of culture in the novel is the encyclopaedia (*Me* 20, 26, 31, 55, 114, 115), which Ramírez reads avidly. As a result, he begins to know *that*, but he still does not *know*, for this can come only from remembering past experiences involving the emotions. The written word is no more than an empty signifier, and this is underlined when the older man observes that Larry might have liked to take home one of the plump pigeons from the section on birds for his cat; unfortunately, though, "los de la enciclopedia son de papel" [the ones in the encyclopaedia are only paper] (*Me* 115). What both of them eventually learn, therefore, does not come from books but from human contact, from the Other. It is no coincidence that in eighteenth-century France, although the *Encyclopédie* was intended to be a "general inventory of extant knowledge, compiled in a purely objective and scientific spirit," and by means of it "lingering darkness was to be expelled by the light of reason," intellectualism was soon superceded by sentimentalism, and the latter movement not only introduced new artistic growths but also, paradoxically, heralded intellectual progress.[52] The heart could not be denied, and it may have proved beneficial to heed it.

Perhaps the existence of hope and faith, which are by-products of the imagination, is best explained by the Buddhist view that desire is the source of illusion; both hope and faith are born of people's unexceptionable wish that their deepest needs be met, and they survive because supporting "evidence" is constantly furnished by the emotions. This is unconnected with what reason and observation tell us, and the "evidence" often flies in the face of external reality. While hope and faith are often directed toward a powerful and benevolent God and the concept of infinity, they may also manifest themselves in an indestructible thirst for goodness, order, and the predominance of

---

51 Hillman, *Emotion*, 175–76.

52 L. Cazamian, *A History of French Literature* (1955; Oxford: Oxford UP, 1960) 217–18.

positive absolutes in everyday life and relationships. This thirst is one of the sources of myth, which, as Elizabeth Janeway observes, "is born out of psychological drives" and "opposes belief to facts in order to change the facts *or obscure them*" (emphasis added).[53] Myth embraces the wish to grasp the secret of the universe but it also signifies the need to be assured of personal survival. More superficially and cynically, it can be seen as the manifestation of pitiful optimism—a vain hope that the here and now will acquire sense and purpose. In any case, belief in the power of love and justice to bring happiness to the individual provides constant sustenance. Both Larry and Ramírez demonstrate Puig's suspicion that if this is repudiated, only bleak sterility remains.

Although the dilemma is particularly evident in this novel, it underpins them all, and there are several allusions to it in works of art that are familiar to the characters. In *The Buenos Aires Affair*, the pitfalls of the opposite world view are highlighted when we are told that the adolescent Gladys's reading matter includes Aldous Huxley's *Point Counter Point* (1928) (*BAA* 38). Ostensibly this allusion points to her cultural maturity, but Huxley's ideology may well have contributed to her unhappiness, which—it might be alleged—is, in fact, caused by her immaturity. Given her circumstances, the book's main character, Rampion (based on D.H. Lawrence), is not an ideal role model. Huxley was convinced that modern society had created more problems than it had solved, and David Daiches claims that, for him, "modern psychological and scientific knowledge had emptied the world of value." He adds, "If we know what causes a state of mind, or our emotional response to music, or our belief in religion, we can no longer respect the effects or regard them as an adequate source of value."[54] Gladys takes this view to romantic extremes. That this choice is also impossible is seen in the fact that the knowledgeable and rational Larry and the emotional Gladys suffer equally.

In narrative situations that involve unavoidable betrayal of one of two beloved people, the outcome is tragically predictable. It is only if the choice is expressed in theoretical terms—particularly if the options are knowledge and emotion—that compromise appears to be possible. However, since not one of Puig's characters manages to achieve a state

---

53 Elizabeth Janeway, *Man's World, Woman's Place* (New York: Dell, 1971) 26.

54 David Daiches, *A Critical History of English Literature*, 2 vols. (London: Secker & Warburg, 1960) 2: 1136.

of equilibrium, it is safe to assume that the author feels that this is all too rare. His creations are either ruled by illusion or, at the other end of the scale, are victims of "la angustia de existir" [existential anguish] (*BAA* 34), lacking in faith and aware of the false nature of their apparent security. For Heidegger this constituted a positive aspect of *Angst*, since "the mood of anxiety offers something like total disclosure of the human condition,"[55] but although it may give rise to a more authentic experience of existence, it is invariably painful. Larry is both expert and victim: he read both Sartre's *L'Être et le néant* (1943) and Camus's *L'Étranger* (1942) during his post-religious phase (*Me* 145, 184), but neither work did anything for his peace of mind, nor was there any improvement in his ability to live comfortably with other people. Indeed, when he talks about reading Sartre, he admits to having enjoyed the beauty of knowledge for its own sake. The topic, he says revealingly, was without importance for him; it was "el movimiento que adquiría, la lógica, la belleza, la arquitectura complicada, la estética" [the dynamism it acquired, the logic, the beauty, the complicated architecture, the aesthetics] that attracted him (*Me* 145). Ironically, the book itself proved an obstacle to family harmony: his interest in it increased his alienation from his uneducated father and his mother assumed that any book containing a chapter called "Le Corps" [The Body] must be pornographic. His emotional reaction to the appealing hedonism of Camus's ideology at least gave him the pleasure of anticipating pleasure, but then knowledge interfered with this too: he discovered that the ideal existence portrayed by the French writer had a substructure of colonial exploitation (*Me* 184). Aldous Huxley once wrote that "intelligence is essential . . . but cannot function properly when it is too often or too violently interfered with by the emotions,"[56] but it is clear that for Puig the converse is equally true. Moreover, Larry's emotional life might have suffered even more harm had he also been aware of the nihilism behind the work. To live up to Camus's claim that the only way to escape mortality lies in suicide, intellectual suicide, or rebellion against the world demands enormous courage and constant, distressing lucidity. Even though a kind of happiness may be achieved—for Meursault in *L'Étranger* is undeniably placid—a state of permanent revolt, with its concomitant

---

55 Referred to by John McQuarrie, *Existentialism* (1972; Harmondsworth: Penguin, 1976) 169.

56 Huxley, *Ends and Means*, 265.

refusal to play the game according to the rules, is not normally compatible with contentment. Others may be hurt, and the process is life-enhancing only for those so abnormally self-sufficient and wilful that they can disregard interpersonal relationships. For the majority of people there seems to be no alternative other than conformity, indulging in Sartrean *mauvaise foi*, and trusting in basic morality, possibly with a theistic foundation. The argument for this is neatly laid out by Huxley:

> the union of virtue and happiness, without which the highest good cannot be realized, must be effected by some power external to ourselves, a power which so arranges things that, whatever partial temporary appearance may be, the total world order is moral and demonstrates the union of virtue with happiness.[57]

For Sartre, *Angst* was to be endured, not avoided. For Puig, the pain of those who are enduring it is a distressing creative stimulus, but equal sympathy is directed toward those who make pathetic attempts to avoid it and, however foolishly, choose to believe in the old myths. Molina (*Ebma*), who quite deliberately suppresses his knowledge of the painful aspects of reality, is more appealing than Valentín (initially another example of how education and knowledge have failed to improve the lot of the individual or of the world), and it may even be true to say that he is marginally happier than the younger man. In her romantic days, Ana (*Pa*), too, was happier and more considerate of the feelings of others than Pozzi has ever been. And the idealistic Gladys (*BAA*) is a more sympathetic character than Leo. She could not be described as happy, but at least she is never prey to the guilt and remorse that assail him. He is a theorist and therefore a thinker; she is a practitioner, an artist, even a visionary. On the wall of his apartment Leo has a *tachiste* painting (*BAA* 21), the encapsulation of bitter recognition of the dark side of life, the omnipresence of death, and the possibility of self-destruction,[58] whereas Gladys thinks of him in terms of the typical colors of Henri Matisse (1869–1954), whose work transcends tragedy and reflects "the artist's God-given capacity to

---

57 Huxley, *Ends and Means*, 280.

58 Haftmann, *Painting in the Twentieth Century*, 1: 345–47.

experience happiness."[59] She is, of course, wrong, but in Schiller's words:

> Nur der Irrtum ist das Leben,
> Und das Wissen ist der Tod.
>
> [Only in error is there life,
> And knowledge is death.][60]

---

59 Haftmann, *Painting in the Twentieth Century*, 78. Matisse once referred to art as a "calmant cérébral" [cerebral tranquillizer].

60 I have also used these lines as the epigraph to the chapter on *Sangre de amor correspondido* in *The Necessary Dream*.

IV

Oppression

POLITICAL AND SOCIAL TYRANNY

PUIG'S VISION OF human beings as victims could scarcely fail to result in sympathetic identification with his characters, and this has not gone unnoticed by critics. "Hombre entre los hombres, el autor no se siente superior a ninguno" [A man among men, the author does not feel superior to anyone], Pere Gimferrer claimed in 1978,[1] but Puig himself had already spoken revealingly on the subject of his affinity with his creations in the important 1972 interview we have referred to several times. He was at pains to deny any demythifying intention; neither, he said, was his aim to deride the illusions or the style of others. Though it would be only to easy to be scornful about the pathetic *cursilería* [vulgar pretentiousness] that colors the attitudes, and therefore the lives, of so many of his characters and their real-life models, he admitted to finding this touching, even—in a way—worthy of admiration.[2] Authorial comprehension is particularly strong in cases where individuals suffer as the result of blatant oppression, whatever its source. *El beso de la mujer araña* points unequivocally to the

---

1 Pere Gimferrer, "Aproximaciones a Manuel Puig," in his *Radicalidades* (Barcelona: Antoni Bosch, 1978) 84.

2 "Yo no condeno la cursilería, me enternece. Mira . . . yo creo que la cursilería está motivada por un afán de ser mejor" [I don't condemn pretentious vulgarity. The fact is . . . I think it's based on a desire for improvement]. Rodríguez Monegal, "El folletín rescatado," 29.

similarity between sexual and political exploitation and their psychological and social consequences. This interchangeability might have been purely literary, with one form of oppression indicating or representing the other, but for Puig the connection is essentially causal. "For me," he has confessed, "sexual oppression is the school of all the others."[3] This does not mean that political tyranny is less important to him than sexual injustice; his own experiences in Argentina in one of its most repressive epochs suggest that both sets of circumstances have autonomous as well as intertextual value.

Some of the cultural references already mentioned underline the position of individuals and groups affected by political or international disputes. In *I Puritani*, we saw that the near-tragedy of the plot is caused by the situation of the Royalists in seventeenth-century England, while in *Nabucco*, it is the Jews who are suffering at the hands of the Assyrians. In *Lakmé*, the lovers' happiness is thwarted because of conditions in colonial India, where two cultures met on an unequal basis. Nearer home, Molina's (*Ebma*) Latin American terrorist film portrays one response to political oppression, and with *Destino*, in spite of the disconcerting emphasis on the superficial appeal of the Nazis (which may also represent masochistic enjoyment of tyranny, according to the theories of Erich Fromm[4]), the reader cannot fail to be reminded of the true conditions in occupied France during the Second World War. Even in Molina's version of *I Walked with a Zombie*, with its telling depiction of a workforce dehumanized by ruthless and corrupt capitalistic despotism, social oppression is a major theme.

The appeal of stories with a background of armed conflict usually stems from the audience's need to be assured of the ultimate triumph of justice and order, as well as from the vicarious excitement to be found in the polarized and often simplistically interpreted values of the situation. Puig, however, uses plots that involve racial and political antagonism in order to highlight man's inhumanity to man: it is the motivation and philosophy behind conflict that is important, not its result or the tension of the action. Even the brief mention of the musical film *Fiddler on the Roof* (starring Topol, dir. Norman Jewison, 1971), which is being shown in Buenos Aires during the years of military rule (*Pa* 165), fits into this category, since this winning-through

---

3 He said this in a taped conversation in 1987.

4 See Erich Fromm, *The Fear of Freedom* (1942; London: Routledge, 1960) *passim*.

story begins when the Jewish hero escapes from Tsarist Russia after a bloody pogrom; there is a more than tenuous connection here with the current situation in Argentina. Furthermore, one of the reasons why Thomas Mann features in *The Buenos Aires Affair* may be so that the reader's awareness of his renowned concern with freedom from tyranny, the horrors of war, and the possible breakdown of civilization may contribute to the atmosphere of a novel in which violence is a major element. It has been claimed that in *Doktor Faustus* (1950), "Germany is Faust, the mixture of genius and madness"; this echoes the contradictory state of Argentina as Ana and Pozzi see it in the later novel, *Pubis angelical*.

One of the most interesting allusions here is to the 1956 Polish film *Kanal* (dir. Andrzej Wajda), which is being shown in the Buenos Aires of the military régime (*Pa* 165). Defeat, it has been said, is present from the very beginning of this account of an anti-Nazi resistance group trapped in a sewer.[5] The great myths engendered by war in general and the Second World War in particular are coldly laid bare, and the impossible choice that faces the desperate victims is horrific indeed. The traditional symbolic significance of light is turned upside down for those whose survival seems to depend on remaining in hiding in a dark and fetid subterranean tunnel, but in fact there is no question of survival, for the action takes place in 1944 and the post-war audience knows that whatever happens there is no hope for them.

As for social oppression, it is probably not fortuitous that the author has one of his unhappiest creations, Paqui, read and enjoy Victor Hugo's *Les Misérables* (1862) (*RH* 181), in this way linking the problems and limitations of the poor in the French novel with those of the most disadvantaged sector of Coronel Vallejos. This is perhaps the most blatant instance of an unlettered character being familiar with a classic text, and the author, aware of the incongruity of this, disarms us by mentioning Mita's astonishment at her friend's choice. The fact that he risks the reader's incredulity with this reference confirms its importance. Where poverty and underdevelopment are concerned, the hopelessness of formulating a plan of action is underlined: in a rigidly hierarchical society, resistance will have to be of the magnitude of the French Revolution, and if the victims are also women, resignation may appear to be the only possibility. In the same novel, Héctor is advised

---

5 B. Urgosikova, *"Kanal," The International Dictionary of Films and Filmmakers*, ed. Christopher Lyon, 2 vols. (1984; London: Firethorn, 1986) 1: 236.

to read *La incógnita del hombre* (*Man the Unknown*, 1935) by Dr. Alexis Carrel, a book that enjoyed great popularity in Buenos Aires in the forties (*RH* 159), but it is difficult to see why he should do so, for, as Juan Comas has observed, in it Carrel "maintains that the proletariat and the unemployed are people who are inferior by heredity and descent—men inherently lacking the strength to fight, who have sunk to the level at which fighting is no longer necessary."[6] Héctor's youthful ambitions will hardly be strengthened by this view. The other, equally popular, book that is recommended to him is *El libro de San Michele* (*The Story of San Michele*, 1929) by Axel Munthe. Since this author's most salient characteristic is pessimism, perhaps Puig's intention in drawing our attention to both works was to highlight the unlikelihood of improvement in his characters' lives.

State despotism and the likely failure of resistance are also brought to mind by Larry's early assimilation of Lenin's *The State and Revolution* (1919, though written in 1917) (*Me* 50, 51), a somewhat overoptimistic vision of the future under communism. By the time the work was published, the October Revolution had deposed a tyrannical system, the Bolsheviks had declared their policy of sexual liberation,[7] and justice for all seemed to be at hand. However, the outcome was a less than utopian society, and in the narrative of the novel it is not long before Larry begins to feel that Marxism is not a panacea for all ills. His disillusion is echoed by the anti-Soviet sentiments of Gladys (*BAA* 43), though her feelings are based less on knowledge or experience than on three works of art: the film *The Iron Curtain* (with Gene Tierney and Dana Andrews, dir. William Wellman, 1948), in which a disenchanted Soviet official in Ottawa reveals information about a spyring to the U.S. authorities (this was based on the real-life defection of one Igor Gouzenko), and two personal accounts of defection to the west: *La noche quedó atrás* (*Out of the Night*), by Jan Valtin, and *Yo elegí la libertad* (*I Chose Freedom*), by Victor Kravchenko. Gladys's ignorance of the subject and the fact that her views come from partial or highly romanticized accounts add another dimension to possible interpretation of these allusions. She is passive and manipulated while Larry

---

6 Juan Comas, *Radical Myths* (Paris: UNESCO, 1951) 10.

7 Peter Fry and Edward MacRae, in *O que é a Homossexualidade* (São Paulo: Editora Brasiliense, 1983), remind us that the new régime abolished the law against homosexuality in 1917, but that there was a backlash in the Stalinist era and a major pogrom in the thirties.

actively studies the subject, but neither of them has found the "right" answer. We have already noted how attitudes toward interpersonal relationships are influenced, if not dictated, by art—"One shouldn't take art too seriously," says a character in Gladys's favorite *Point Counter Point*[8]—and political philosophy, documentaries, and auto-biography are forms of art, even if they confidently purport to present us with the "facts."

Chronologically, Gladys is not the first Puig character acquainted with Thomas Mann, for in *La traición de Rita Hayowrth*, Toto lends a copy of *The Magic Mountain* (1924) to Herminia (282). She finds it impossibly long, and from this can be inferred the superiority of Toto's intellect and taste in spite of his youth. However, there are further implications, including the similar circumstances of Toto—personally isolated in an isolated environment—and the novel's hero, Hans Castorp, whose period in a sanatorium is dedicated to a traumatic process of self-discovery. What is relevant in the present context is Castorp's connection with the First World War. Like the resistance fighters in *Kanal*, both his options are pernicious: he can stay enclosed in an alienated and morbid world or he can go down from the mountain and rejoin life. In the event, he chooses liberty, and ironically, it is the war that frees him.[9] His "liberation" is therefore highly ambiguous; there is every chance that he will die in battle, and as the book ends, the hope that love will reassert itself is patently groundless.

Puig's novels constantly draw our attention to individuals who are in the power of others. The exploitation of the poor by the rich, the weak by the strong, women by men, and children by parents (particularly fathers) is, at least partly, the result of inflexible adherence to social norms, class hierarchy, and apparently immutable gender stereotypes. The victims can, of course. rebel against tyranny, but references to those who have challenged established régimes or social systems are not encouraging. If the oppressed choose to revolt rather than accept the status quo, they will—as in so many other areas of life—have to disregard both history and fiction.

---

8 The speaker is Philip Quarles.

9 Henry Hatfield, *Modern German Literature: The Major Figures in Context* (London: Edward Arnold, 1966) 95.

THE JEWS

Only Puig's more attentive readers will have noted his allusions to the Jewish predicament throughout history, for not one of these is to be found in the narratives; certainly they have gone unremarked by critics. However, although they are symbolic rather than specifically referential, they may be judged important since they underscore the themes of marginality, victimization, and exile.

The subject of the oppression of the Jews is explicit in two very different works, which are granted only a passing reference: the opera *Nabucco* and the musical *Fiddler on the Roof*. Even less obtrusive, but possibly effective at a subconscious level, are the resonances of the Holocaust in Second World War stories like *Kanal*, and further equally subtle references, one of which is to Emil Ludwig (1881–1948), whose books appeal so much to Mita (*RH* 147). Some readers might know that Ludwig's real name was Cohn and that he was a Jewish refugee who originally came from Breslau. Then, Lion Feuchtwanger (1884–1958) is referred to in *The Buenos Aires Affair*; though his name crops up only once, his writings do contribute to Gladys's education, and it may be relevant that he lived in forced exile in the United States.

Jews are not always sympathetically portrayed in fiction, and when they are shown as cruel and avaricious they can serve the same symbolic purpose as evil women: both groups represent a threat, and emphasis on their alleged misdemeanors will provide justification for their persecution. The character of Shylock is indirectly conjured up when *The Merchant of Venice* is mentioned in *La traición de Rita Hayworth* (85), and the Jews are also depicted as predatory and sinister in *Destino* (*Ebma* 55 *et seq.*). Although the point of the reference to the Shakespeare play is to underline Toto's cultural pretensions (he is lying when he claims to have seen it), his ignorance of its orientation might also imply that, as a child, he has yet to be conditioned by divisive social and religious prejudices. The emphasis on the Nazi view of the Jews in *Destino* cannot fail to remind us of the horrific consequences of anti-Semitism.

Female and Jewish threats to society come together in Jorge Isaacs's *María*, a favorite novel among some of the Coronel Vallejos women (*RH* 146, 181, 186, 187, 194). Its popularity stems from its twin themes of female suffering and eternal male devotion, but as Sharon Magnarelli has so rightly noted, there is much more to it than that, for the eponymous heroine suffers a double conversion.[10] Long before her lover turns her into an appropriate object of his affections, she is converted from Judaism to Christianity. Her original name had been Ester, recalling the biblical personification of the spirit of revenge and the isolationism that persecution provokes, and it may also be relevant that Queen Esther's ultimate triumph was born of deviousness and the power that beauty bestows. However, like so many dangerous women, María's potential is defused—long before she is old enough to make a decision for herself—and she is recuperated. Efraín, her latter-day Ahasuerus is not now at risk. With her natural aspect suppressed,[11] she subsequently exists only as a foil to the hero, and on her death he converts her into the counterfeited memory of a counterfeit existence. María is no more than an absence all the way through the novel, for her unreformed, anarchic presence would have constituted an intolerable danger to an inflexible—and, it could be alleged, insecure—social system.

EXILE, ISOLATION, POVERTY, DEATH

A sense of the isolation of all Puig's protagonists cannot be avoided, and this is reinforced by cultural references to individuals who, for various reasons, are removed from familiar surroundings. The classic example is found in *La traición de Rita Hayworth*, when, for no apparent reason, the reader is informed that Toto has presented a young friend with a copy of *Robinson Crusoe*. On reflection, the parallel becomes clear: both Defoe himself (a non-conformist and a dissident) and his creation (who finds himself virtually alone in a hostile environment) echo Toto's own situation. Furthermore, Robinson Crusoe's strategy for survival is not dissimilar to the child's; as David Daiches has so aptly put it, "he improves what is there."[12]

---

10 Magnarelli, "The Love Story: Reading the Writing in Jorge Isaacs' *María*," chapter 1 in *The Lost Rib*, 11–37.

11 At first she is described in terms taken from nature and her name also suggests the goddess Ishtar, who is closely related to Venus and vital continuity. In this context, too, there is a kind of mutilation as she is assimilated into Christian society. When the influence of Romantic literature is added to the teachings of Catholicism, she is at last fit to form part of the Christian patriarchy.

12 Daiches, *A Critical History of English Literature*, 602.

It is surely no accident that so many of Puig's creations are in exile since Puig himself spent a great many years away from Argentina. The situation is reflected in the narratives by Gladys and Leo (*BAA*) (for part of their lives, at least), by Ana (and the *Ama* and W218) (*Pa*), by Ramírez (*Me*), by Luci and Nidia (*Cnt*), and also—in a way—by Toto (*RH*), and Josemar (*Sac*), who has abandoned a rural background in order to make his way in the world, only to end up in abject urban poverty. Supporting these situations are allusions to Thomas Mann, Emil Ludwig, Lion Feuchtwanger, and Herman Hesse; to two Russian dissident authors; to the hero of the film *The Iron Curtain*, the Israelites in *Nabucco*, the heroine of Molina's version of *I Walked with a Zombie*, and the Empress Carlota in the film *Juárez* (admired by Toto and Mita); to the character played by Marlene Dietrich in *Shanghai Express* (also starring Clive Brook, dir. Josef von Sternberg, 1932) (*BAA*, epigraph to chapter 4); to the *Tres argentinos en París* [*Three Argentines in Paris*]— which was actually called *Tres anclados en París* [*Three People Stranded in Paris*][13]—(*Bp* 140), and to Albert Camus's *L'Étranger*.

Poverty is a form of banishment too, and Herminia (*RH*), Josemar (*Sac*), and María José and Ronaldo (*Cnt*) are among those who are never allowed to lose sight of this fact. However, the greatest tyranny and the most oppressive cause of ontological isolation is death: "Dios mío, qué solos / se quedan los muertos!" [Dear God, the dead are so alone!] as Bécquer observes in the poem that haunts Clara Evelia (*BAA* 11). (In the same novel, Leo's posthumous, futile ejaculation illustrates and emphasizes this concept.[14]) In Puig's unpublished play already referred to, death is stressed again when one of the characters says: "Nacemos y morimos solos. A lo largo encontramos a quien nos acompaña, por momentos. Y eso es todo" [We are born and we die alone. Along the way we find somebody to keep us company for short periods. That's all there is to it]—not, of course, a highly original idea, but one that it is essential to bear in mind when interpreting the

---

13 "Anclao en París" [Stranded in Paris] is also the title of a well-known tango by Enrique Cadícamo, with music by Guillermo D. Barbieri, which was recorded by Carlos Gardel in 1931.

14 The importance of this detail is confirmed by the fact that it was invented by the author. It is not mentioned in the source material for the autopsy report in *The Buenos Aires Affair*: two chapters, "Método general de autopsia" [General Autopsy Method] and "Autopsía legal" [Legal Autopsy], from *Autopsias*, by Felipe A. Vivoli, which were with Puig's notes for the novel.

author's work. It applies to everyone: the varying levels of sophistication and learning in the characters are unimportant, for, as Northrop Frye has claimed, "every mind is a primitive mind, whatever the varieties of social conditioning."[15] On a collective level, distress in the face of extinction is alleviated by the myth of the Eternal Return, but tales of heroic resurrection and rebirth fail to comfort those conditioned by Romantic individualism.

In "The Ego and the Id" (1923), Freud wrote that if life consists of a continuous descent toward death, it is the claim of Eros, of the sex drive, that holds up the falling level and introduces fresh tensions. In Puig's novels, romantic love, a refined—perhaps perverse—development of this drive, acts as a short-term defense against a fundamental sense of solitude. For the majority of the characters it is essential to believe in its existence and efficacy, in the face of all the odds; Erich Fromm's judgment that "to feel completely alone and isolated leads to mental disintegration, just as physical starvation leads to death" is only too relevant here.[16] A human being is a victim, and once again this view is often expressed in melodramatic terms: there is unremitting emphasis on undeserved suffering in the cultural quotations, which audiences recognize, even in exotic or unlikely narrative circumstances. Puig's protagonists are searching for eternal values, and for many of them these are confirmed in art founded on Romantic premises, particularly the cinema. As Frank McConnell has put it:

> Romanticism and its child, film, represent a rupture of the ancient self-assurance of human intelligence, represent the coming-of-age of that intelligence to a sense of its isolation from the rest of the world and, therefore, to the terrible necessity to return—if only in dream—to the rhythms of that world.[17]

The distance between individualism and self-centredness is dangerously small, but it is worth repeating that the author never condemns those who dwell in a world of illusion, even if this might be judged a form of primary narcissism. Indeed, for him illusion is

---

15 Northrop Frye, *The Great Code: The Bible and Literature* (1981; London: Routledge, 1983) 37.

16 Erich Fromm, *The Fear of Freedom*, 15.

17 Frank D. McConnell, *The Spoken Seen: Film and the Romantic Imagination* (Baltimore: Johns Hopkins UP, 1975) 182.

essential to human existence; he understands that to live is to be incomplete, oppressed, and victimized, and that the artistic correlatives of the objects of human desire are life-enhancing, especially when romantic love is their basis. This view is supported by Erich Fromm when he maintains that "love for man cannot be separated from the love for one individual. To love one person productively means to be related to his human core, to him as representing mankind." And this is vital, for "human solidarity is the necessary condition for the unfolding of any one individual."[18] When this happy state is achieved, the pain of subjection to oppressive power is diminished. (With so many other factors to be taken into consideration, it is unlikely to be eliminated.) The problem, as Puig sees it, is that the male sex so seldom fulfils Fromm's criteria for "productive" love; women seem to be so much more capable of the care, responsibility, respect, and knowledge that he deems essential.[19] Even if tyranny is not an exclusively male province in real life, the vast majority of the examples alluded to by Puig can be attributed to *macho* men. An intensified example of man's inhumanity to man is men's inhumanity to women. However, belief in at least some degree of improvement is essential to human well-being; like Fromm, Manuel Puig believed that without faith we become sterile, hopeless, and afraid to the very core of our being, with a consciousness of death that cannot be suppressed.[20]

According to Julia Kristeva's theories on foreignness, "as soon as foreigners have an action or a passion, they take root. Temporarily, to be sure, but intensely;"[21] metaphorically, this judgment can be applied to ontological "exiles" too—that is to say, man. However, the incompatibility between the kind of life-enhancing actions or passions experienced (perhaps chosen) by Puig's characters and any improvement in their social circumstances is only too obvious. If, as Kristeva maintains, "the foreigner . . . can only be defined in negative

---

18 Erich Fromm, *Man for Himself: An Enquiry into the Psychology of Ethics* (1947; New York: Fawcett, 1969) 107.

19 Fromm, *Man for Himself*, 104 *et seq.*

20 Fromm, *Man for Himself*, 201.

21 Julia Kristeva, *Strangers to Ourselves*, trans. Leon S. Roudiez (New York: Columbia UP, 1991) 5. (Originally *Étrangers à Nous-mêmes*, Paris: Fayard, 1988.)

fashion,"[22] romantic illusions furnish a positive element, but at the same time they perpetuate some of the circumstances that add to human suffering.[23]

---

22 Kristeva, *Strangers to Ourselves*, 95.

23 In *The Fear of Freedom*, Erich Fromm defines as "neurotic" the person "who has not given up fighting against complete submission, but who, at the same time, has remained bound to the figure of the magic helper, whatever form or shape 'he' may have assumed" (54). And he condemns "the cheap and insincere sentimentality with which movies and popular songs feed millions of emotion-starved customers" (211). There is little doubt that Puig's protagonists are neurotic, but even if their faith in the values of all kinds of culture is misplaced, it is unquestionably touching.

V

The Search for Identity

NATIONALISM AND CULTURAL DEPENDENCE

IT WOULD BE TEDIOUS, as well as unnecessary, to list all those who have elaborated theories on the subject of the internal divisions that disturb and inhibit the individual. Philosophy, psychology (particularly psychoanalysis), religious studies, sexology, and psychiatry, as well as areas of literary analysis that have recourse to these disciplines, are permeated by speculation about the contradictions found in the psyche. If to be human is to be divided, then the struggle for a unified identity is the most universal preoccupation of all.

Adler was in the minority in his lack of sympathy toward any exaltation of a sense of personality, which he saw as compensation for an inferiority complex; most other theorists have assumed that consciousness of personal fragmentation leading to feelings of inadequacy exists in the majority of people to a lesser or greater degree. Unhappiness is the inevitable result. Not infrequently this condition is found on a collective level, especially among nations made up of recent immigrants. Puig once commented sympathetically on the search for national identity in his native Argentina:

> En mis novelas me he ocupado principalmente de una primera generación de argentinos, los hijos de los inmigrantes españoles e italianos que llegaron al país a fines de siglo. Se trataba en general de campesinos que venían aquí a hacer fortuna, a cambiar de *status*. Las tradiciones que podían aportar no valían, eran tradiciones de campesinos, una identidad que convenía olvidar. En el caso de los inmigrantes italianos, era peor: ni siquiera pudieron aportar un idioma a sus hijos.

. . . Y los hijos no eran ni italianos ni españoles, eran argentinos, pero no sabían cómo era ser argentino.

[In the main I have devoted myself in my novels to first-generation Argentines, the children of Spanish and Italian immigrants who arrived in the country at the turn of the century. They were mostly country people who came here to make their fortunes, to try to improve their social standing. Any traditions they brought with them were worthless, they were the traditions of rural people, and this was an identity it was better to forget. Where the Italian immigrants were concerned it was worse: they couldn't even provide their children with a language. . . . And the children were neither Italian nor Spanish, they were Argentine, but they didn't know what being Argentine meant].[1]

Some years later he remarked that even North Americans share this problem, which he defined as "una cierta búsqueda de la identidad" [a kind of identity search].[2] If "Who am I?" is the most pressing universal question, it is even more apparent in those who lack the security of longstanding socio-political and cultural systems and traditions.

Despite the close links between national identity and national culture, the quest for these takes place in different areas: the first in the field of politics, the second (though insidious political influence is inevitable here too) in the world of the arts, whose axis, for developing countries, has inevitably been located elsewhere. Both aspects of this quest are explicitly depicted in almost all of Puig's novels. Only *Sangre de amor correspondido* ignores the topic altogether, and this is because its setting is so limited and poor that the characters are completely unaware of the outside world. Although Josemar wears a *Volta-do-Mundo* [Round-the-World] T-shirt and enthuses about travel as a

---

1 When he made this statement (in "El folletín rescatado"), only *La traición de Rita Hayworth* and *Boquitas pintadas* had been published.

2 Pérez Luna, "Con Manuel Puig en Nueva York." As always, Puig understood the point of view of those with whom he disagreed. In "Chistes sobre argentinos / El último tango en Venezuela," he claimed that behind what he called their "máscara de arrogancia" [mask of arrogance], Argentines were concealing "una profunda inseguridad" [a deep insecurity]. He then sympathetically pointed out that although no other country has fought so hard to emerge from "ese subdesarrollo latinoamericano que pareciera imposible superar" [Latin American underdevelopment, apparently impossible to overcome], Argentina has failed to do so.

means of expressing the independent, *macho* temperament that he does not, in fact, possess, he has no conception of what this means or what he would find if an opportunity were to present itself. All the other texts are colored by the Argentine political situation, particularly the influence of Peronism. It has been claimed that these could be classified as historical novels,[3] with emphasis on what Unamuno designated *intrahistoria*: in them we discover what daily life in a given period was like, and cultural references clarify the picture.

A characteristic of the Perón régime, especially in its first phase, was emphasis on national identity. In the early forties Perón made no secret of his admiration for the Nazis and the fascists (writing in 1956, Ernesto Sábato referred to the "estructura espiritual hitlerista" [Hitlerite spiritual structure] of Peronist indoctrination[4]) and the word "fascist" was not infrequently employed by Perón's adversaries.[5] The admiration of the *Conductor*[6] for the Italian system was expressed in public on more than one occasion,[7] and among the elements of European régimes imported into Argentina were concentration camps (for a short period, at least), anti-Semitism (which Perón unconvincingly repudiated), a Gestapo-style secret force called the *Control* (*del Estado*), torture, and the suppression of civil liberties. Behind all these was the Argentine version of the nationalistic attitude of German national socialism. Clearly, this was very likely to appeal to a population conscious of its lack of roots; indeed, in 1946, when the United States published the famous "Blue Book," reporting on Argentina's pro-Nazi

---

3 See, for example, Gimferrer, "Aproximaciones"; Juan Goytisolo, "Manuel Puig: una novela política," *El viejo topo* (Supplement "Libros," December 1979), and my "The Projection of Peronism in the Novels of Manuel Puig," *The Historical Novel in Latin America: A Symposium*, ed. Daniel Balderston (Gaithersburg: Ediciones Hispamérica and The Roger Thayer Stone Center for Latin American Studies, Tulane University, 1986) 185–99.

4 Ernesto Sábato, *El otro rostro del peronismo: Carta abierta a Mario Amadeo* (Buenos Aires: Imprenta López, 1956) 29.

5 For example, Perón's 1948 constitutional changes were dubbed "the fascist reform" by the Argentine Socialist Party. See George Blanksten, *Perón's Argentina* (Chicago: U of Chicago P, 1953) 75. Blanksten claims that, in fact, the régime was always more fascist than Nazi.

6 Puig uses Perón's title, *Conductor*, for Hitler in *Destino*, the Nazi propaganda film recounted by Molina in *El beso de la mujer araña*.

7 See Blanksten, *Perón's Argentina*, 164.

activities, this increased Perón's popularity among his followers, for their natural resistance to foreign interference was by this time turning into rampant xenophobia. Perón actually designated his new policies "the nationalist revolution,"[8] and although in later years circumstances obliged him to retreat from his antagonistic stance vis-à-vis the United States and other foreign countries, his contribution toward a sense of Argentine identity, even in his political enemies, cannot be disregarded.

The presence of Peronism becomes more and more explicit with each new Puig novel,[9] until in *Pubis angelical* it is discussed in detail by the protagonists, one of whom, Pozzi, is a dedicated member of the party. However, even before this its influence is noticeable. One example is the school-text purple prose of Gladys's *sensación*, in which she equates national and personal fulfilment (*BAA*); another, the equally pompous style of the diary of Esther, the recipient of a Peronist education grant (*RH*).

The reader's awareness of nationalism is increased by several specific references. For instance, there is nothing unusual about the fact that schoolchildren are required to read their country's classic literature (that Héctor [*RH*] is supposed to read Esteban Echeverría is a case in point), but what is ironic is that it was Echeverría who, with missionary zeal, first introduced European Romantic conventions and ideas into Argentina, and these were incompatible with current Argentine reality and the dogmas of the dictator Juan Manuel Rosas (who assumed power in 1829). In Echeverría's short story "El matadero" [The Slaughterhouse] (c. 1840), the essential civilization/barbarism opposition is only too evident, to the extent that Jean Franco has concluded that the text suggests that "in the slaughterhouse of Argentina only the worst elements thrive."[10]

Héctor's *macho* character is made up of many of the motivating elements of barbarism. Conditioned patriotism is also indicated when, in the same novel, the poem "Patria" [Native Land] is recited (*RH* 35), but at the same time the variety of surnames throughout the whole

---

8 Blanksten, *Perón's Argentina*, 222.

9 For a view of the importance of this element in the novels, see my "The Projection of Peronism."

10 Jean Franco, *An Introduction to Spanish-American Literature* (Cambridge: Cambridge UP, 1969) 50.

range of Puig's characters (Casals, Etchepare, D'Onofrio, Druscovich, Pozzi, Ramírez, etc.) suggests the extent of the difficulty in achieving any sense of nationhood. In *Boquitas pintadas*, when Mabel is dismissive about Argentine films (*Bp* 140), the national dilemma is emphasized. Hers, it seems, is a typical stance; Molina (*Ebma*), with his love of tangos and boleros, is one of the few Puig characters with any regard at all for Argentine cultural products. The others are admiringly dependent on other countries—either unadulterated, as with European literature, opera and Hollywood films—or in the form of imported values, such as those that pervade Jorge Isaacs' *María* and everything that Esteban Echeverría ever wrote.

Argentines are faced with a choice that is peculiar to their kind of society as well as with universal problems: their options are to reject foreign cultural intervention and influence in the attempt to forge a distinctive identity, or to accept and enjoy these and, in so doing, take the risk of inhibiting and distorting their culture's individuality. The dilemma is reflected in one aspect of the political choice that had to be made in the forties. Even though Puig was strongly anti-Peronist, he had some sympathy for certain aims of the movement in its first phase. He evidently felt that there was something to be said for the claim that "muchísima gente buena se hizo peronista" [a large number of good people became Peronists] (*Pa* 57) in those early years. Undoubtedly, Perón's most praiseworthy objective was to improve the lot of ordinary people, but the efforts he made to inculcate a feeling of national solidarity were bound to provoke condemnation as well as approval, even within Argentina itself.

Role models from alien cultures have been the only possibility for developing countries, and these are often—if not always—politically suspect, though their admirers are unable to perceive this. All they see are higher standards and greater professionalism in imported works of art, never realizing that the question of standards is open to debate and that professionalism has no connection with ethics. Consumers are thus manipulated, even exploited. The poor are entertained and instructed by cultural products that represent the ideology of the rich; the white races act as paradigms for the non-white; an urban life-style is presented to rural communities for emulation. Europe and the United States have often provided incongruous models for Latin America.

As Puig's characters reveal, the value of Argentine culture is judged in relative terms: Buenos Aires is enterprising and civilized because the opera is as good as in Bayreuth or Parma (*Pa* 192), because the *porteños* recognized Ingmar Bergman's talents so quickly (*Pa* 167), and because they were among the first to appreciate the theories of Lacan. Eurocentrism is underlined when we discover that at a given moment, under Lanusse, they could attend concerts given by The English Chamber Orchestra, The Loewengath String Quartet, and The Promusica of New York, or they could go to see the play *Yvonne* by the Polish writer Witold Gombrowicz (*Pa* 166):[11] all this in addition to the programs of foreign origin offered by countless cinemas.

Unsurprisingly, cultural dependence is a constant in the allusions to works of art: there are very few that are Latin American, much less Argentine. Clara Evelia constantly plays the music of Handel, Sibelius, Mussorgsky, Beethoven, and Albéniz during her pregnancy (*BAA* 29): perhaps one of the author's reasons for choosing this particular group is that they are all considered representatives of their own countries (always assuming, of course, that Handel is thought of as English). At the same time, her pen-name, "Ariel"—reminding us of the cohesive effect of *arielismo* on Latin America[12]—and her admiration for Latin American poetry indicate that she is being pulled in two different directions. Europeans stay within their cultural traditions (it is not fortuitous that the Spanish soprano Victoria de los Ángeles sings Spanish music at her Buenos Aires recital), but Latin Americans are cultural colonials. This is underlined when we are told that the Chilean pianist Claudio Arrau plays Bach, Mozart, and Chopin at his concert, and that the Ballet de la Ciudad de Buenos Aires will be dancing to the music of Stravinsky (*Pa* 165).

Almost everything of importance is exotic: Gladys's values are culled from *Harper's Bazaar* (*BAA*), the great man whose name graces Toto's school is George Washington (*RH*), and in *Pubis angelical* the year 1948 is evoked by songs made famous by the French singer Charles Trenet (*Pa* 152). Of course, since there is a relatively sparse national heritage to draw on, Latin Americans have always had little option but to look elsewhere. Furthermore, they themselves have ensured the continuation of the colonizing process by insisting that knowledge of alien cultures is a sign of sophistication and superior

---

11 Gombrowicz, who lived in Argentina from 1939 to 1963, always considered himself an *émigré* writer, and this was one of his favorite topics.

12 José Enrique Rodó's essay *Ariel* (1900) led to a certain sense of solidarity among Latin American intellectuals. Though Clara Evelia is devoted to foreign music, her reading will obviously have to be in Spanish.

social class. Only the poor, uneducated, and underprivileged, it seems, live in the enclosed artistic world of the tangos and *rancheras* played at the *romería* in *Boquitas pintadas*, with titles such as "El Entrerriano" and "Mi rancherita" (*Bp* 98–99), or, like Josemar (*Sac*), of the sentimental songs of the Brazilian Roberto Carlos.

Even if all this is regrettable, even absurd,[13] it is yet another dilemma that is virtually insoluble. Insistence on supporting *lo nacional* is almost certainly counterproductive. In *La tajada*, set in 1944 and 1950, the topic is aired when a Peronist minister justifies his current defense of the Argentine cinema—which he had earlier claimed was "porquerías" [rubbish]—by saying: "Lo defiendo porque es argentino, pero es malo" [I stand up for it because it's Argentine, but it's rotten just the same]. It was "malo" in the epoch because it was trying to be something it was not and to do something it could not do well. In the novels, there are even hints that hybridization can be disconcerting. For example, the music that makes the *Ama* uncomfortable (in what is obviously Xochimilco) is pseudo-oriental, neither one thing nor the other (*Pa* 130, 133): it is *Scheherezade* by a Russian (Rimsky Korsakov), *Lakmé* by a Frenchman (Delibes), and *In a Persian Market* by an Englishman (Albert Ketelbey). Condemnation is also implicit in the mention of a "rumba hollywoodizada" (*Pa* 114), a counterfeit version of the Cuban dance. Then, at least some readers may be struck by the absurdity of a double transculturation—the imitation of an imitation—when, in a Latin country, LKJS takes W218 to a nightclub with an artificial "palmar de cocoteros bajo cielo estrellado y tropical, al son de maracas y bongós" [coconut palm-grove beneath a starry tropical sky, with the sound of maracas and bongo drums] (*Pa* 187): a tropical copy of "The Coconut Grove."

This specifically Latin American impossible choice was actually made many decades ago, and unless Argentina now emulates post-Revolution Cuba and creates a whole new society based on a different ideology, it seems unlikely to be reconsidered with any rapidity. Even if national cultural attitudes are in the process of changing, European judgments are still valued. Pozzi, for example, quotes the British *Daily Telegraph*'s view of Perón as a "laborista del subdesarrollo" [an under-

---

13 For an entertaining account of growing up with alien cultural influences, see Luis Rafael Sánchez, "Apuntación mínima de lo soez," *Literature and Popular Culture in the Hispanic World*, 9–14. See also "Culture in the Age of Mass Media," spec. issue of *Latin American Perspectives* 16, V, 1 (1978).

developed country's version of a Labour Party leader] (*Pa* 120). The attitude summed up in the well-known Portuguese phrase *para-inglês-ver* [for the benefit of the English] is slow to disappear. The transculturation that is a fact of Argentine life is evident in two of Puig's own titles: *La traición de Rita Hayworth* (in which one of the many explanations of the word "betrayal" could be culturally based, for the style of Hollywood is unattainably alien), and *The Buenos Aires Affair* (which connotes the English detective story genre).[14]

It takes centuries for a new nation to find out who it is, always supposing that this is a possibility. Much has been written on the collective problems of the immigrants to Argentina since the turn of the century, including many tango lyrics and plays by Armando Santos Discépolo. More recently, the Argentine writer Mario Szichman has investigated the question of belonging in a novel in which the theme is highlighted every time a young member of a Jewish family that is trying to learn to be Latin American[15] regains consciousness after a blackout and asks where he is, who he is, and what he is called.[16]

IDENTITY AND GUILT

The difficulties involved in any attempt to establish a homogeneous and autonomous individual identity would appear to be insurmountable; this was certainly the view of Jacques Lacan, who emphasized the need for liberation from the desire for completeness.[17] One of the socially imposed aspects of the search for a unified image that is relevant in any consideration of Puig's novels is emphasis on sexual self-definition. Jeffrey Weeks is among those who have questioned its validity and drawn our attention to its dangers. He points out that since sexual definitions are historically formed, they are "sites of

---

14 Another example of a hybrid title is *Goodbye obelisco*, which Nené and her husband see on their Buenos Aires honeymoon (*Bp* 150).

15 This seemed the only way for them to avoid the pressures of anti-Semitism.

16 Mario Szichman, *A las 20:25, la señora entró en la inmortalidad* (Hanover, NH: Ediciones del Norte, 1980). (The title reproduces the radio announcement of the death of Evita Duarte de Perón.)

17 Lacan refers to the need for analysts to question "the objective status of [the] 'I', which a historical evolution peculiar to our culture tends to confuse with the subject." "Aggressivity in Psychoanalysis," *Écrits*, trans. Alan Sheridan (London: Tavistock, 1948) 23.

contradiction and contention, and can therefore be changed. . . . The seeking out of a 'true identity,'" he adds, can be "a threat and a challenge, because it is the negation of choice. It claims to be finding out what we *really* are, or should be. Its reality is of restriction and force." He goes even further, claiming that security in one's sexual identity may in the end be "no more than a game, a ploy to enjoy particular types of relationships and pleasures."[18] Puig agreed with this point of view, claiming that a sense of identity should never be based on sexual orientation.[19] On a non-sexual level, too, an individual ought to be able to accept oneself as a particular combination of often anomalous constituent elements; the ideal is expressed by Erich Fromm's judgment that "the mature and productive individual derives his feeling of identity from his experience of himself as the agent who is at one with his powers."[20] However, mature and productive people are never found in Puig's fiction, and here the ideal is at least partly dictated by long established social rules, many of them based on gender stereotypes.

The same principle applies where morality is concerned. It is not just a question of being entirely male or entirely female, with all the social and behavioral restrictions that this dichotomy entails, but also of being conditioned into seeing oneself as wholly good or wholly bad. Rare indeed is the person who is unaffected by simplistic moral laws and external judgments. In Freud's view, the human conscience, the superego, is born of the injunctions and prohibitions of the social system. Not everyone agrees. Fromm, for example, finds the theory limited and unsatisfactory, and comments that if it is true, "conscience . . . is nothing but internalised authority."[21] I contend that Puig's texts reveal a certain sympathy for the Freudian thesis: the author clearly thinks that unnecessary guilt feelings are obstacles to individual contentment. At the same time, he is well aware of their potency, and this confusion constitutes another motive for self-analysis, which, in its turn, increases the desire for unity.

In fact, Puig's characters are constantly analyzing themselves, either directly or by means of imaginative projections. This is best il-

---

18 Weeks, *Sexuality*, 181, 188.

19 In a taped conversation in August 1987.

20 Fromm, *Man for Himself*, 80.

21 Fromm, *Man for Himself*, 43.

lustrated in *Pubis angelical*. The text can be divided into two sections: the explicitly investigative principal narrative, with the hospitalized Ana talking and writing about herself, and the stories of the *Ama* and W218, in which she implicitly examines her options. However, it is not just *Pubis angelical* that deals with the problem of identity—the lives of Toto and Herminia (*RH*), Nené and Mabel (*Bp*), Gladys and Leo (and Clara Evelia) (*BAA*), Molina and Valentín (*Ebma*), Ramírez and Larry (*Me*), Josemar (*Sac*), and Silvia (*Cnt*) are all quests for self-knowledge; significantly this list includes both the educated and the uneducated, the intellectually enquiring and those of limited curiosity, young and old, male and female. For Freud, psychoanalysis was a means of achieving health; Puig's creations feel that self-analysis is a step toward happiness. Perhaps the two concepts are synonymous.

However, as we saw in the case of Ana (*Pa*), there is no guarantee that self-recognition will not be a misrecognition, and the complexity of this problem is stressed by supporting references. Sometimes these provide the source of a character's self-image, sometimes they reflect it; they may represent an ideal, or they may act as an ironic authorial comment on what the character believes to be the truth. Their contribution to the texts is therefore a major one, and much is lost if they are overlooked. One of the most subtle examples of how illuminating a cultural allusion can be is the point in *La traición de Rita Hayworth* when the reader is told that, alone among his friends, Toto is fascinated by the film *Spellbound*. In his analysis of this, René Alberto Campos has shown how the plot echoes the child's inner turmoil and guilt, as his conflict with paternal/superego authority increases.[22]

If Toto's identification with the hero—and, according to Campos, the heroine—of *Spellbound* is the most subtle allusion to a character's condition, it is the referential function of the terrorist film in *El beso de la mujer araña* that is the most unusual. This is because the imagination from which the details spring is not that of its protagonist; here, for much of the time at least, Molina is conducting an investigation into Valentín's identity. This is just as likely to be inaccurate as self-analysis, since Molina's reading and "recognition" of his cellmate are dictated by his own experiences, attitudes, feelings, and prejudices. Like all psychoanalysts, he imposes himself on his patient (one of the reiterated complaints against Freud was that he confused the problems of his own particular society with those inherent in human existence),

---

22 Campos, *Espejos*, 87 *et seq.*

and the reader has to judge the extent to which his conclusions are subjectively based. Like any author, he is creating an identity within his own emotional and ideological parameters. Moreover, his terms of reference are largely taken from the field of psychoanalysis, which itself has become inflexibly authoritative. It was Foucault who claimed that the psychoanalytic institution has now become a site of power/ knowledge that simultaneouslyoorganizes and controls.[23]

In this context, too, it is impossible to make a fruitful choice. The orthodoxy behind sexual and moral self-analysis—which is almost certainly suspect—forces the individual into limiting categories and may result in guilt and alienation. On the other hand, if we are to judge from Puig's creations, it is unlikely that modern man will be persuaded to abandon a search for identity.

EMULATION

Emulation of others is a normal part of the human growing process, but when adults choose role models from alien and unrealistic contexts it can be classified as escapist fantasizing. Many would challenge Freud's sweeping judgment that "happy people never make fantasies, only unhappy ones,"[24] but its aptness cannot be doubted where Puig's characters are concerned. One after another of them has recourse to the imagination in an attempt to evade a reality that is at best unappealing and at worst intolerable. The first stage in the process consists of superficial imitation of other people, and the aim—which is seldom articulated, since the subject is usually unaware of the purpose of the exercise—is to acquire the model's presumed advantages and happiness, to "become" this person. This is a variation of Otto Rank's "counter-will": "wanting at the level of what others have or want,"[25] but in Puig the gulf between the subject and the Other is often so vast as to be ludicrous. What adds to the absurdity of the situation is that his characters can have no knowledge of the true circumstances of their real-life models—one thinks of Herminia's admiration for Mrs. Abraham Lincoln (*RH*)—but, what is (perhaps) worse, many of them copy fictional creations.

---

23 Quoted by Weeks, *Sexuality*, 176–77.

24 Freud, "Creative Writers and Day-dreaming," *SE* 9 (1908).

25 Otto Rank, *Truth and Reality*, trans. Jessie Taft (1936; New York: Norton, 1978) 63.

One of the most pathetic instances of the emulation of a person whose real circumstances are entirely unknown is found in *La traición de Rita Hayworth*, where Choli has a sense of affinity with the Argentine actress Mecha Ortiz because she mistakenly assumes that she too is a widow.[26] Then there is Clara Evelia's desire to be like Alfonsina Storni and Juana Ibarbourou, who were actually so dissimilar (*BAA*), and Herminia's determination to emulate Schubert because she cannot see further than the beauty of his music (*RH*). And the consequences of Ana's identification with the beautiful Hedy Lamarr (*Pa*) are only too obvious.

Emulation of those who exist only on the stage, the screen, or the written page is not without its sinister element, for their creator's ideology is often unthinkingly accepted. Unhappy, even desperate, people are persuaded to want what others decide they should want. It is difficult to know whether paradigms taken from highbrow art or those from the mass media are the more dangerous, for although the latter have a wider and (probably) less perspicacious audience, the apparently unassailable stature of the former is a distraction, and their insidious influence may be equally harmful. In any case, at least on the basis of Puig's writings, there is little point in distinguishing between the two, for the educated and the uneducated are influenced by both. Furthermore, there is little variation in the stereotypes that they contain. Gladys (*BAA*) is well read, travelled, artistic, talented, and sensitive, but this does not prevent her from trying to live up to the impossible female image proposed by the magazine *Harper's Bazaar*.

Incongruity is taken to its extreme when Molina's *loca* friends model themselves on Greta Garbo, Marlene Dietrich, Marilyn Monroe, Merle Oberon, Gina Lollobrigida, and Hedy Lamarr (*Ebma* 272). Here we have men imitating women, Argentines imitating North Americans or Europeans, and—even more important—(fictitious) real people imitating (real) fictitious people. They admire, and identify with, women who do not actually exist, who are merely actresses, interpreters of the products of the imaginations and ideology of others. Actors became indistinguishable from their stereotyped roles in the Hollywood star system because of efforts made by the studios of the period to project a consistent image. The result, in René Alberto Campos's words, was

---

26 The actress's husband, who spent more than twenty years in a mental hospital after suffering head injuries in a riding accident, did not die until 1948. See her autobiography, *Mecha Ortiz* (Buenos Aires: Editorial Moreno, 1982) 30.

a "juego de máscaras y apariencias" [a game of masks and appearances], something that "de partida era falsa" [was bogus in the first place].[27] Molina and his companions see themselves as women of incomparable beauty who behave nobly in tragic and melodramatic circumstances: Garbo in *Grand Hotel*, reacting stoically when John Barrymore is killed (dir. Edmund Goulding, 1932) (*BAA* 45 and epigraph to chapter 15), or in the last scene of *Camille*; or Dietrich, who is forced into espionage in *Dishonored* (also starring Victor McLaglen, dir. Josef von Sternberg, 1931) (*BAA*, epigraph to chapter 13), and into prostitution in *Shanghai Express* (with Clive Brook, dir. Josef von Sternberg, 1932) (*BAA*, epigraph to chapter 4). However ludicrous the relationship may be, it is socially and psychologically significant that this marginalized group's "camp" view of their own situation should be accurately reflected in subservient, frustrated, suffering feminine images.

Puig said on more than one occasion that he originally intended the protagonist of *El beso de la mujer araña* to be female, but changed his mind because he realized that contemporary women have seen through the myth of *machismo*.[28] This position is also reflected by the *Ama*'s hard-earned acquisition of the ability to read men's minds at the age of thirty (*Pa*). Nevertheless, in spite of the rational views expressed by the author in interviews, his fiction demonstrates a certain lack of conviction on the subject. In the first place, there is the question of generation, and the conditioning that is hard to erase. When, for example, Ana's other self—or her daughter—W218, acquires supernatural perspicacity at twenty-one without having to go through a period of disillusion, the story is set in the future. For the present, not just *locas* but also many women continue to espouse traditional values. Then, because of Puig's overwhelming sympathy toward his characters and his total understanding of what inspires them, the reader may suspect that he shares their enthusiasm for values and styles that he simultaneously challenges. Writing about the footnotes in *El beso de la mujer araña*, Roberto Echavarren has rightly suggested that one of their most important functions is to highlight the gulf between "una homosexualidad 'posible' y 'el modelo reducido' de la homosexualidad de Molina"

---

27 Campos, *Espejos*, 163.

28 This assertion has always struck me as being totally implausible, unless the author originally planned a very different plot and setting for the novel. Though I never asked him about this, I found no evidence for it among his notes.

[how homosexuality could be and the 'limited model' of Molina's homosexuality],[29] and there is an equally wide gulf between women's traditional position and their unrealized potential. Yet Molina is one of the most consummate, human creations of twentieth-century fiction, a character with whom the author unquestionably feels a strong affinity, in spite of his emulation of the "wrong" models. Among the unavoidable (postmodern) inconsistencies to be found in Manuel Puig is his simultaneous adhesion to social progress (expressed explicitly in interviews and implicitly in his fiction) and his love of the threadbare values that console his characters.

PSYCHOLOGY, PHILOSOPHY, NATURE

Despite the best efforts of those who, like Borges, attempt to persuade us to the contrary, it seems that mankind will never accept the idea that there is little point in trying to comprehend anything. Curiosity, dissatisfaction, and faith in the possibility of improvement in the human condition are irrepressible. In the contemporary world, where neither religion nor rationalism reigns, psychology, together with what has been designated its most powerful and comprehensive system, psychoanalysis, has become one of the most valued tools in the search for solace through understanding. Since the figure of Freud still dominates this system, it is likely that his emphasis on the libido will invite modern man to judge sexual equilibrium an important element in his struggle to live at peace with himself and the world.

Puig's fictional creations are distinguished by their inability to achieve any semblance of peace: their distress is either sexually based, or—as in the case of Valentín (*Ebma*)—it is exacerbated by problems arising from their sexuality.[30] Fromm has commented that "many people today expect books on psychology will give them prescriptions on how to attain 'happiness' or 'peace of mind,'"[31] and among these are at least some of Puig's characters. It is to one of the most promin-

---

29 Echavarren, "*El beso de la mujer araña*," 75.

30 Valentín has an ambivalent attitude toward his mother. Moreover, the demands of his ideology are incompatible with his emotions and desires. For Freud and many of his disciples political radicalism was a sign of neurosis, since "the liberal bourgeois was the paradigm of the healthy man." Erich Fromm, *Greatness and Limitations of Freud's Thought* (London: Jonathan Cape, 1980) 134.

31 Fromm, *Man for Himself*, vii.

ent post-Freudians, Jacques Lacan, that Ana (*Pa*) turns in her quest for identity and contentment, and this choice is not without irony, since her interest in his theories is born of her subservience to Pozzi. Here we have two examples of the continuing power of the superior man: that of her ex-lover, and that of an influential male theorist. Her ultimate (and suspect) self-recognition is therefore still the result of accepting "la mirada de los demás" [the gaze of others] (*Pa* 171). Her newfound approach to life may or may not prove fruitful, but the perceptive reader may suspect that she has moved out of one area of misrecognition into another.

The psychological footnotes in *El beso de la mujer araña*, like all the other quotations, act as a commentary on the characters' condition and development, but it would be a mistake to overlook the distinguishing effect of their extradiegetic nature; the consciousness and voice behind them come directly from the author and they make no claim to represent the thinking of either of the protagonists. The process of selection of the points that are made is, of course, important and revealing, but what is even more significant is that the last cited authority, the Danish sexologist Dr. Anneli Taube, is a woman, and that, furthermore, she does not actually exist. The ideas attributed to her are Puig's own.

After considering some of the work that has been produced over the years on the causes of homosexuality, and refuting some common misconceptions, the notes focus on the subject of the social norms that oblige some people to repress or disguise their sexuality, and this process, together with salient points taken from Anna Freud's theory of over-repression and the danger of impotence, frigidity, and guilt complexes, is the common denominator that runs through all the novels. For example, Choli (*RH*) finds intercourse distasteful because of the incompatibility between current romanticism and carnality. Leo (*BAA*) is both impotent and guilt-ridden because of the strict sexual discipline of his early childhood. Ana (*Pa*) is an amalgam of the two, for her loss of interest in sex soon after her marriage is surely the result of the moralistic romantic views that have been inculcated in her. The notes go on to cite Freud's view that the heterosexual couple cannot be a universal ideal, and this underlines the absurdity of Molina's desire to be a bourgeois "wife." It seems that we are moving toward some kind of solution to the frustration and unhappiness of the characters, and we are given a hint as to its nature in the mention of infant bisexuality.[32] The theories of "Dr. Anneli Taube" confirm this impression: they constitute a plea for universal acceptance of the fact that humankind is both male and female, and for revised behavior patterns.[33]

Although this sketchy résumé implies that the arguments lead consistently to the final message, the reader is likely to have reservations regarding some of the authorities quoted, especially as the theories of at least two of these have been widely questioned, if not discredited, since the heyday of their popularity and influence. These are Herbert Marcuse and Wilhelm Reich, two of the gurus of the generation that fought for sexual liberation in the sixties, a movement described by Jeffrey Weeks as "a god that failed."[34] Its utopianism left behind it a sense of disillusion, radical feminists saw its philosophy as male-oriented and exploitative, sociologists classified it as a largely upper middle-class phenomenon, and many deplored the fact that the most influential theorists ignored such important issues as friendship between members of the same sex, romantic love, and homosexuality.

Ambivalence toward the notes is intensified when Puig acts as his own devil's advocate, referring, for example, to the equation of sexual liberty and social decadence. This is yet another point in the texts at which the author is signalling the complexity of a problem rather than indicating its solution. While there is little doubt that he believed in the advantages of accepting the principle of bisexuality, I suggest that he could not avoid the realization that it would be unlikely to prove a universal panacea, even if people could be persuaded of its value. Perhaps unwittingly, he invites the reader to consider the views of Michel Foucault, who has written about the impracticality of the sexual ideology of the sixties. Though admitting that the liberationist doctrine "a fait rêver d'une autre cité" [has inspired dreams of a different city],

---

32 This, of course, stems from Platonic theory.

33 For further comments on these footnotes, see Yves Macchi, "Fonction narrative des notes infrapaginales dans *El beso de la mujer araña* de Manuel Puig," even though this critic makes the very dubious claim that "le texte B [the footnotes] n'éclaire en rien le texte A [the narrative]" [text B sheds no light whatsoever on text A] (68). See also Juan Manuel García Ramos, *La narrativa de Manuel Puig. (Por una crítica en libertad)* (La Laguna: U de La Laguna, 1982) chapter 2; and my *The Necessary Dream*.

34 Weeks, *Sexuality*, 13. See also George Frankl, *The Failure of the Sexual Revolution* (London: Kahn & Averill, 1974).

Foucault points out that both sexuality and knowledge can be modified only at considerable cost. He goes on:

> Il faut donc s'attendre que les effets de libération à l'égard de ce pouvoir repressif soient lents à se manifester; l'entreprise de parler du sexe librement et de l'accepter dans sa réalité est si étrangère au droit fil de toute une histoire maintenant millénaire, elle est en outre si hostile aux mécanismes intrinsèques du pouvoir, qu'elle ne peut manquer de piétiner longtemps avant de réussir dans sa tâche.

> [Where this repressive power is concerned, one must therefore expect the effects of liberation to be slow in manifesting themselves; any undertaking to talk freely about sex and to accept it as it is is so alien to the mainstream of our entire history, now a thousand years old, and, furthermore, is so opposed to intrinsic power mechanisms, that it will incontrovertibly have to mark time for a good deal longer before it succeeds.][35]

The choice for Puig appears to be one between continuing to accept a largely repugnant system and working to change it through increased understanding (Foucault's *volonté de savoir*). However, we have also noted in the narratives that the need to know can also constitute a form of futile oppression. In *Maldición eterna a quien lea estas páginas*, Larry's peace of mind is disturbed rather than increased by the acquisition of knowledge, for understanding entails confronting the dark side of the self. This is illustrated in several of the texts. The Praxiteles statue of Hermes (*BAA* 204–05) suggests perfect beauty, but this god has a further aspect. Although he is—as Joseph Campbell puts it—"the great figure of the guide [and] the teacher," he is also "the conductor of souls to the afterworld."[36] It could be argued that all life is a journey toward "the afterworld," but the emphasis on the moment of departure—that is, death—is explicit in that Hermes is often depicted as the ferryman who transports departing souls.

The presence of death and its connection with the sexual drive permeate Puig's writings, and even if it can be claimed that his interest in

---

35 Michel Foucault, *Histoire de la Sexualité: La Volonté de savoir* (Paris: Gallimard, 1976) 12, 15, 17–18. When I discussed Foucault's theories with the author in 1987, he claimed that Foucault ignores the fact that we can have no conception of the nature of a sexually satisfied world.

36 Joseph Campbell, *The Hero with a Thousand Faces* (1949: Princeton: Princeton UP, 1968) 72.

Freudian theory tends to be usurped by acceptance of Otto Rank's will psychology in the later books (especially in *Sangre de amor correspondido*),[37] he never loses sight of Freud's judgment that Eros and the death instinct are related.[38] Humanity's great capacity for destructiveness can be directed toward the self. Fromm maintains that this tendency can be ignored only by means of superficial wishful thinking, and goes on to elaborate on the nature of the impossible choice implicit in this, asking how the destructive side of mankind's nature can possibly be curbed without sanctions and authoritative commands.[39] Since so many of these are challenged by Puig, it is inevitable that he should present the human situation as one of extraordinarily difficult solution. The *beso* is fatal for the *mujer araña* herself,[40] as Molina always knew it would be. His identification with Irena in *Cat People*, as well as with her medieval prototype, is not gratuitous. Gladys's involvement with the protagonist of Hesse's *Demian* (*BAA*), who does achieve emotional equilibrium, should be read as an example of Fromm's "superficial, wishful thinking," as her later life sadly proves. In Puig's view, man is not just a victim of others, but also of himself, and for the latter condition there may be no remedy.

The quest involves a desire to understand the nature of the world as well as of the self, with countless philosophical systems the result. Larry (*Me*) is one of those who look for answers in philosophy, as we have already seen, but in vain. When the novel opens he has not only stopped trying to locate some intelligibility in life but to all intents and purposes has stopped living. Puig appears to be suggesting that philosophy itself can be alienating, for it seems to promise something that it ultimately fails to provide, even though students may persuade themselves that they have found a complete answer. Crippling disillusion will set in when it is discovered that it is not, as had been hoped, a therapeutic area of study. In Larry's case, knowledge of Marx, Hegel, and existentialism has not contributed to his equilibrium. It goes without saying that neither the devaluation of the individual in Marx-

---

37 For an interpretation of this text based on Rank's theories, see my *The Necessary Dream*.

38 Freud, "The Ego and the Id," *SE* 19 (1923).

39 Fromm, *Man for Himself*, 215, 216.

40 In his musical version of the novel (which was ultimately rejected), Puig created a new film story: in it, a baby girl is cursed at birth to kill anyone who later falls in love with her.

ism nor Hegel's idealistic theory (that everyone is absorbed into an absolute transcending personality) is likely to provide comfort for a confused, unsure person conditioned by individualism, but his study of existentialism might have proved more promising. After all, Heidegger's philosophy involves *Grundbefindlichkeit*, a fundamental process of "finding oneself." Furthermore, some have maintained that a certain contentment can be achieved if the causes of *Angst* are understood and Sartrean *mauvaise foi* rejected. However, Larry's situation indicates the author's scepticism about the level of happiness resulting from an exclusively cerebral approach.

Yet another option seems to be the recovery of primitive man's sense of unity with nature, but in this context, as in so many others, the purity of the desire has been contaminated, both by sentimentality and by imposed values. The former leads the fictional characters to eschew reality. As for the latter, nothing could be more reasonable than a desire to regain the capacity to recognize and cope only with external natural enemies, since the modern alternative also involves the enemy within and hostile elements in civilization,[41] but in Puig's novels it is not just a question of yearning for prelapsarian innocence and unadulterated beauty: primordial nostalgia has been distorted by unacceptable elements from the patriarchal superstructure. It is, perhaps, not surprising that the cultural references that indicate this particular aspect of a blind determination to see things as they are not are all associated with women.[42]

The mention of Gabriela Mistral (*BAA* 32) in connection with Clara Evelia reminds us that nature was one of the two predominant themes of this poet, and that this would have an immediate appeal for the ingenuous would-be poet; moreover, Juana Ibarbourou, with whom Mistral is bracketed in the novel, was often called "the child of nature." In *La traición de Rita Hayworth*, it is a naïve young girl, Teté, who talks about St. Francis of Assisi, and the eponymous heroine of Mita's favorite novel, *María*, is described by means of natural, essential

---

41 See Rank, *Truth and Reality*, 48.

42 The only allusions to nature in Puig's narratives—in *Sangre de amor correspondido*—deconstruct Josemar's *macho* self-image. For interpretations of the natural symbolism, see Elías Miguel Muñoz, "*Sangre de amor correspondido* y el discurso del poder judeo-cristiano," *Revista Iberomaericana* 130–31 (1985): 73–88, expanded in *El discurso utópico de la sexualidad en Manuel Puig* (Madrid: Editorial Pliegos, 1987), and my *The Necessary Dream*.

terminology before she is converted. Then, the effeminate Toto's connection with Robinson Crusoe suggests a relationship with nature, in contrast to the *macho* Héctor's refusal to read *El libro de San Michele*, a text which also emphasizes this.

According to Jean Baudrillard, primitive people were entirely without a sense of alienation,

> car le sujet n'est aliéné—comme nous le sommes—que lorsqu'il intériorise une instance abstraite, venue de l'arrière-monde, comme disait Nietzsche—psychologique (le moi et l'idéal du moi), religieuse (Dieu et l'âme), morale (la conscience et la loi)—instance inconciliable à laquelle tout le reste est subordonné

> [for the subject becomes alienated—like us—only when he interiorizes an abstract call from the ulterior world, as Nietzsche called it— whether this be psychological (the ego and the ego-ideal), religious (God and the Soul), or moral (conscience and the law)—a call which is irreconcilable and to which all else is subordinated].[43]

However fatuous the world view of many of Puig's female characters may seem to be, these women (and we should include Toto in this group) form part of an important modern syndrome, for in the first five decades of this century literary primordialists constantly articulated the quest for innocence and unity. The difference between writers like D.H. Lawrence, Octavio Paz, and certain poets of the Spanish '27 Generation and Puig's fictional characters is the difference between people who have worked out a philosophy that can be tested (and that was roundly condemned by many[44]) and those who unthinkingly find unrealizable illusions essential. Like so many forms of escapism, the regressive attitude of the fictional characters is wishful thinking. The tree and the water of life were lost with the Garden of Eden, and the only possible direction is forward. However, it cannot be denied that Puig sympathized with this attitude, and in this context, yet again, he demonstrates the superior sensibility of "the illogical feminine."

The facile nature of the beliefs of Puig's women is indicated in the epigraph to chapter 3 of *The Buenos Aires Affair*, which consists of dialogue from a film that echoes Gladys's search for a successful amalgam of beauty, natural innocence, animality, and glamor in her life, a search

---

43 Jean Baudrillard, *L'Échange symbolique et la mort* (Paris: Gallimard, 1976) 216.

44 For example, by de Rougemont, *Passion and Society*.

that is doomed to fail because she never challenges an ideological framework that includes so many mutually incompatible elements. *La princesa de la selva* ([*The Jungle Princess*], with Dorothy Lamour and Ray Milland, dir. William Thiele, 1936) is the story of another child of nature who finds fulfilment by means of love. This simplistic situation stands in chilling contrast to the tragic circumstances of the novel's heroine, but, yet again, there is no element of condemnation in Puig's treatment of her.

The curse of alienation began, according to Baudrillard, with "l'intériorisation du Maître par l'esclave émancipé" [the interiorization of the Master by the emancipated slave].[45] His mutually incompatible *maîtres*, as we have seen, are those of all mankind, and there is little hope of eradicating internal divisions. Neither psychoanalysis, philosophy, nor vague primordialism can provide the key to the transcendental perfection of the Gospel according to St. Thomas:

> Jesus said unto them: When you make the two one, and when you make the inner as the outer and the outer as the inner and the above as the below, and when you make the male and female into a single one, so that the male will not be male and the female not be female, when you make eyes in the place of an eye, and a hand in the place of a hand, and the foot in the place of a foot, and an image in the place of an image, then shall you enter the Kingdom.

However, this metaphysical text does point to a partial solution for society: the reduction in the rigid differentiation that is a major theme in Puig. On an accidental rather than a constitutional level, change is possible. The question remains whether, deep down, the author was prepared to face up to the risks that change involves. Social reform based on the revaluation of women benefits both sexes, since in addition to eradicating one area of social injustice our obsession with personal identity may be diminished, but his fascination with the individualism of his characters suggests that, for him, this would entail loss as well as gain.

---

45 Baudrillard, *L'Échange symbolique*, 217.

VI

Harsh Reality

BENEATH THE SURFACE of all the novels lies dualism: the Platonic distinction between the temporal and the eternal; the Cartesian separation of mind and body; ethical dualism (which contrasts facts and value judgments); explanatory dualism, with its challenge to the principle of cause and effect; and even epistemological dualism (differentiating between perceived and inferred objects). The surface itself consists of situations and characters that exemplify these divisions (the importance of which, I contend, Puig never doubts), and the reader cannot fail to become aware of his implicit desire for fusion, or, when this is patently impossible, for a more tolerable balance. The sub-themes based on these dualisms, such as the internal male-female division, emotional as opposed to cerebral bases for views and behavior, the flesh and its apparent incompatibility with the spirit, and the co-existence of good and evil within the same individual (with the unpredictability of the Other an important consequence), do suggest that there is some possibility of choice between limiting polarizations. Though it is generally assumed that choices should be informed, Puig suggests that self-knowledge, and clearsightedness in general, can actually be a barrier to happiness.

In addition to those implications already considered, too much information can inhibit relationships, as illustrated by Larry (*Me*). His realization that he is both bad and good, weak and strong, foolish and perceptive, results in the loss of illusion, and he no longer has faith in concepts such as the good wife or the wise man, the self-sacrificing mother or the trustworthy friend. His scepticism is partly attributable to an exaggerated estimate of his own percipience but, more important in this context, it is also due to the self-hatred that facing up to his own duality has engendered. Those characters least prone to self-analysis and almost entirely dependent on their emotions (that is to say Puig's female creations) are seldom suspicious about the integrity and motives of others. (Ana [*Pa*] eventually becomes an exception to this.[1]) Suppression of any recognition of their own internal contradictions means ignorance of the potential duplicity of those that they depend on, of the fact that, as R. D. Laing observes, we are all agents who can, and do, destroy the humanity of others.[2]

Facing up to the truth about ourselves may have destructive implications for religious faith too: the dialogue between God and His Son in *Maldición eterna a quien lea estas páginas* reveals the author's conviction that it is man who has created God in *his* image; cynicism and mistrust therefore affect the human vision of the Almighty. Even consolatory belief in a benevolent fate is likely to be undermined by the smallest trace of self-hatred, since this concept is as firmly underpinned by moral conditioning and the philosophy of just rewards as any religion. The world view of oppressed but virtuous women in Puig's novels, as well as that of the characters in the fictions they so often allude to, confirms this. Yet again, it seems that if there is any choice regarding a world view, the options are equally discomfiting.

One of the darker aspects of society is made up of poverty, class distinction, and hierarchical cruelty. These may be largely, if not entirely, attributable to exploitative human avarice and lust for power, and as such should be challenged and resisted, but it is easier for victims to believe in predetermination, to wait for a stroke of good fortune, and to avoid dwelling on injustice. Mita's amazement that anyone might wish to read Hugo's *Les Misérables* (*RH* 181) is born of this attitude: it is depressing to consider the plight of the destitute,

---

1 In his last novel, *Cae la noche tropical*, the author returns to the theme of voluntary blindness. Silvia, an apparently perceptive psychologist, has every right to be disillusioned with love, but is not. "Aunque sea a una balsa me subiría con él. Una balsa que no lleva a ninguna parte. O que sí lleva." [I would even go off on a raft with him. A raft that isn't going anywhere. Or perhaps it is.] (*Cnt* 219).

2 R.D. Laing, *The Politics of Experience* (Harmondsworth: Penguin, 1967) 25, 11.

since nothing can be done about it.[3] Social determinism cannot be challenged any more than the force of destiny.[4] To quote Laing again, it is commonly thought that humans are subject to "forces from the stars, from the gods, or . . . *forces that now blow through society itself, appearing as the stars once did to determine human fate*" (emphasis added).[5] However, Larry (*Me*) illustrates the danger of taking the opposite stance. His recognition of life's bitterness—something Mita, for example, never openly admits to—stems in part from his awareness of social injustice. Puig's lack of conviction on this subject is evident when, by means of a cultural reference, he implies that this may not have been its only source. Larry, of course, claims that his disillusion with the hedonism of Camus's *L'Étranger* sprang entirely from his distaste for the novel's colonial setting, but it may also have been fuelled by the lack of emotion in the novel's hero, Meursault: his indifference when his mother dies, his coldness toward a sexual partner, his callousness when he witnesses the ill-treatment of a dog. Larry faces up to the harshness of reality, even to the knowledge that he himself contains the root of evil: he is aware that darkness exists without *and* within. The consequence is that when Ramírez ultimately diagnoses the younger man's condition, he is incontrovertibly right: Larry has given up all feeling in order to avoid shame (*Me* 248).

Another Puig character who embodies the theory that internal and external evils are interdependent is Leo (*BAA*). In this context too his *tachiste* painting (*BAA* 21), which I have already referred to, subtly reinforces the dark side of the novel and of life. Wols (Otto Wolfgang Schulze), perhaps *tachisme*'s most important figure, was obsessed by

---

3 The perceived consolatory function of literature was even more explicit in the first draft of *La traición de Rita Hayworth*. In it, Mita also wonders why anyone would want to read Thomas Mann's *The Magic Mountain*, or anything at all by Dostoyevsky: "Se amarga la gente" [One becomes bitter], she claims. This does not appear in the final version of the novel.

4 In *Maldición eterna a quien lea estas páginas*, Larry's virtually illiterate father was brought up in poverty, then spent his life struggling to make a basic living (*Me* 145, 206). Nevertheless, he had no desire to reform society; as for Marxism, his son claims that "él habría sido el último en interesarse" [he would have been the last person on earth to take an interest in it], and that he just wanted to get out of the working class (*Me* 223).

5 R. D. Laing, *The Politics of Experience*, 25. Needless to say, Laing finds this creed totally unacceptable.

chaos, persecution, poverty, homelessness, and perpetual flight. Werner Haftmann says of his work that "whenever life appears, the aura of death is also present," and points out that it contains an all-pervading hatred of sex.[6] I am convinced that, given the connection made by Harold Rosenberg between Action Painting (which includes *tachisme*), the artist's psyche, and European existentialist thought, Puig's passing reference to the school is not fortuitous.[7]

There may also be implications in the mention of Fellini's 1967 film *Histoires Extraordinaires* [Extraordinary Stories], which Leo dismisses on the grounds of its pretentiousness (*BAA* 152). This may be no more than an indication of Leo's discernment, but it is worth remembering that the best-known of the *histoires* was a version of Edgar Allan Poe's short story "William Wilson" (1839). This account of a man with a sinister double is a perfect example of what Keppler has designated "the mystery of a contradiction of simultaneous distinction and identity, of an inescapable two that are at the same time an indisputable one." This double is a "real" second self—that is, he possesses external reality and is independent of the subject, but the two share a basic psychic identity. They are "preoccupied with each other, affect each other [and] exist for each other."[8] The relevance of the Poe tale lies in the fact that the double is actually the protagonist's virtuous half; when this is destroyed, only evil remains. There may be an authorial hint that Leo's life is going in the same direction, and once more the ambiguous morality of Hermes is relevant. Then, in the same novel, when Puig tells us that the exhibition that the optimistic Gladys refuses to attend is of the works of Georges Rouault (1871–1958) (*BAA* 72), this piece of information is surely not gratuitous, for Rouault's paintings are full of the bitterness that is born of human, rather than aesthetic, experience, and they were executed by a man who judged

---

6 Haftmann, *Painting in the Twentieth Century* 1: 345, 346. He refers to "the prevailing despair in human nature [also manifested in the work of Pollock and Tobey] which seemed capable of the most unconscionable crimes" (347).

7 See Angela K. Westwater, "Action Painting," *The Fontana Dictionary of Modern Thought*, eds. Alan Bullock and Oliver Stallybrass (London: Fontana–Collins, 1977) 6.

8 C.F. Keppler, *The Literature of the Second Self* (Tucson: U of Arizona P, 1972) 1, 9–10, 12.

the world "the realm of Satan."[9] Although Gladys's utopianism does her no good, Rouault's world view has little to recommend it either.

BETRAYAL

Of all Puig's themes, betrayal is the most obtrusive. The narratives are replete with treachery, and the fact that it so often appears to be unavoidable suggests that the author judges human beings doubly helpless, born to be the dupes of others, and themselves forced by uncontrollable circumstances into the role of deceiver. It may be that a certain responsibility for both these circumstances lies with the individual, for in the end all betrayal is the result of the false nature attributed to the Other, to ideologies, or to ideals: a further instance of misrecognition. However, given Puig's sympathy for those who are nurtured by illusion, he would have been unlikely to see this explanation as fruitful even if he recognized its validity.

One area that cannot be overlooked is that of misleading appearances. Rita Hayworth in *Blood and Sand* (*RH*) is the most striking example in the texts of perfidious human beauty: her behavior serves to confound the equation of beauty with virtue, which underpins early cultural experiences such as the reading of fairy stories, and which can even permeate those of later life when it reappears in romantic fiction, film, and the visual arts. However, once disabused, the subject's reaction is likely to be a search for inner beauty. The heroines of *The Enchanted Cottage* (*Ebma*) and *Marianela* (*RH*) exemplify this, and the concept is a source of solace for Molina and for some of the female inhabitants of Coronel Vallejos. The danger, of course, is that since art has always tended to deal in polarizations, the equally untenable counter-myth that equates virtue with plainness may well hold sway. Toto is incontrovertibly betrayed by Rita Hayworth, but Molina is equally misled by his faith in the redemption of the "sirvienta fea" [ugly servant-girl] of *The Enchanted Cottage* with whom he identifies. A clearsighted, demythifying approach that would repudiate both simplistic positions would seem to be the answer.

This would inevitably lead to a more authentic view of existence, but Puig's texts suggest that it is not only art that deals in polarizations, but also the human psyche. Not for the first time the relationship between attitudes and culture has to be classified as circular, each

---

9 Haftmann, *Painting in the Twentieth Century*, 1: 78.

continuously giving rise to the other. Though longstanding myths are by no means immune to challenge, their rejection is considered undesirable by the majority of Puig's characters. As his references to works of art demonstrate, the survival of many of these myths is ensured by the universal popularity of those cultural products that espouse and perpetuate them. Primal needs may even be served by their conservation: though Western man constantly questions value systems, it is not only in primitive and archaic societies that myth can be judged "the very foundation of social life and culture," in Mircea Eliade's words.[10] Psychological needs may remain unheeded if fantasy is rejected.

In the present context, the sexual element in myth creation should not be disregarded. The link between physiological and psychological drives needs no elaboration, and with sexual attraction the most basic human desire is often converted into faith. Romantic love calms all fears, for the lover invests the desired object with virtue. This, perhaps, is the only antidote to that distrust of the Other that stems from self-knowledge/self-hatred and that, as we have just seen, is so well exemplified by Larry (*Me*), who has lost the capacity to love.[11]

The essentially positive nature of beauty makes the repudiation of myth difficult, for one of the motives for the creation of myth is a longing for beauty. It could be alleged that in Puig's world the kind of beauty that is admired and desired is artificial, ephemeral, and bogus. The demythifying argument would indubitably advocate a move away from the appreciation of what is patently superficial and frivolous, such as the upswept hairstyles that delight Molina (*Ebma*), the perfect makeup of the supposedly primitive heroine of *The Jungle Princess* (*BAA*), and the "boquitas pintadas" and the intoxicating perfume of the New York blondes (*Bp*). This seems eminently sensible, but it is impossible to live outside one's epoch, divorced from its standards and fashions, and the continuity of observational and imitative cultural formation in children—even if each new generation does eventually modify social taste—cannot be dramatically interrupted. Toto (*RH*) exemplifies this when, to please his father, he *decides* to admire Rita Hayworth, even though he cannot identify with his father's motives. In this context, to condemn the kind of beauty sought after by society is irrelevant and unhelpful. What is important is that

---

10 Mircea Eliade, *Myths, Dreams and Mysteries* (1957; London: Collins, 1972) 23.

11 See my *The Necessary Dream* for more on this character.

the desire to which fluctuating aesthetic standards respond is an integral part of living.

Seductive women are by no means the only treacherous manifestations of the absolute in Puig; there is no shortage of characters who place their trust in what is ostensibly wholesome and true, stimulating and consoling—in a word, beautiful—only to be disillusioned. Yet they refuse to learn from these experiences. What they have gained from them, it seems, is more valuable than authenticity. Kant's well-known claim that the contemplation of the form of a beautiful *thing* gives one an intuition of life within oneself can surely be extended to include dedication to beautiful concepts. Virtually all philosophical writing on aesthetics, whether supporting the objective or the subjective position, confines itself to the plastic arts, to objects, but many of its propositions are equally applicable to conceptual beauty. Kant's "pure pleasure," for example, which is achieved when the mind finds rest and peace in itself, is essentially shortlived and there is often a subsequent sense of betrayal, just like positive experiences within the life-enhancing areas of love and friendship. Here, as in aesthetics (though the choice is infinitely more important), there are two options: to believe in the possibility of brief glimpses of the sublime, or to see this faith as yet another human fiction.

It could be argued that betrayal comes even sooner when beauty is attributed to what is obviously unworthy. That anything, or anyone, could be classified in this way by demythifying theory is reminiscent of aesthetic objectivism, which maintains that judgments are either right or wrong. The question of variations in aesthetic judgment was dealt with by Hume in his essay "Of the Standard of Taste,"[12] where he accounted for anomalies by pointing to defects in the individual. Where conceptual beauty is concerned, however, both subject and object are defective, and there can surely be no question of right and wrong. The subjectivist position in aesthetics, summed up by the old adage that beauty is in the eye of the beholder, is much more appropriate here. If aesthetic value is determined by personal reaction, human desire and need dictates—and therefore creates—the value of the Other. As we saw in chapter I, although the eponymous heroine of *Turandot* claims that Prince Calaf's name is Love, his motives may have been less selfless than she imagines. This attitude of trust can

---

12 David Hume, *Of the Standard of Taste, and Other Essays*, (Indianapolis: Bobbs Merrill, 1965).

lead to disaster (another instance is Nidia's betrayal by Ronaldo in *Cae la noche tropical*), but the alternative is sterility. Either feelings and intuitions have to be trusted, or a perceived source of beauty must be rejected. Ana's counterpoint scenarios in *Pubis angelical* illustrate the nature of this choice: even though both involve treachery and lead to death, one at least contains the beauty of love and trust.[13]

When a character in Lope de Vega's play *Fuenteovejuna* (1614) asks: "¿Qué es amor?" [What is love?], the answer is "Es un deseo / de hermosura" [It is a desire / for beauty], and this is actually creative: "Beauty is the lover's gift," says Congreve in *The Way of the World*. The resulting happiness, often based on self-delusion, may prove short-lived. Even so, this short but happy dream[14] is life-enhancing, not least because love transforms the lover as well as the beloved. The love affair in *The Great Waltz* (*RH*), like that in *The Enchanted Cottage* (*Ebma*), is a "miracle" (we recall that the Spanish title for the latter film was *Su milagro de amor* [Their Miracle of Love]), which consists of the transformation of the lovers into people aware of their own inner beauty.[15] Like life itself, this awareness is ephemeral ("You are no longer handsome when you've lost your lover," to return to Congreve, "your beauty dies upon the instant"[16]), and the consequent disillusion constitutes a double betrayal, for the beauty in the lover dies with that of the beloved. This echoes the double genitive in the title of Puig's first novel (though only in the Spanish original[17]), and emphasizes the mutuality of personal relationships.

However, though people die, true love does not have to, as is shown by Molina's friendship with Valentín (*Ebma*), which is born of the need to betray him. His reference to Sparafucile, the professional assassin in Verdi's *Rigoletto*, is a background pointer to the impossibility of trust between two people (*Ebma* 25). In Rigoletto's famous aria, "Pari siamo!" [We Are Two of a Kind!], the jester reflects on the fact that whereas Sparafucile kills with the sword, he uses words to

---

13 See my article "Superior Men and Inferior Reality" for more on Ana's dilemma.

14 The last words of *El beso de la mujer araña* are: "Este sueño es corto pero es feliz" [This dream is short but happy].

15 René Alberto Campos makes this point when writing about *The Great Waltz. Espejos*, 102.

16 Congreve, *The Way of the World* (1700). The speaker is Mirabell.

17 Lucille Kerr also comments on this in her *Suspended Fictions* 27–28.

the same end. Molina's identification with Rigoletto constitutes a glimpse of the repulsive in himself, but then his love for Valentín develops, and he becomes aware of his own potential beauty, reflected in that of the plain servant-girl in *The Enchanted Cottage*. Molina's ennoblement as a lover and (as he sees it) Valentín's as the beloved are eternalized in death. For all the artificial superficiality of Molina's mass media role models and, indeed, the practical futility of his sacrifice, beauty is shown as a valid concept.

Betrayal is also a commonplace in contexts in which the sexual factor is less obtrusive, one of these being the family. In all the novels, the ideal of disinterested affection and harmony is shown as being an illusion: Toto's relationship with his father, his mother's disappointment in him (*RH*), Choli's critical attitude toward her son (*RH*), Nené's aversion to both her boys (*Bp*), Gladys's contempt for her mother and Clara Evelia's hatred of her (*BAA*), Valentín's ambivalence toward his mother (*Ebma*), Ana's peculiar attitude toward Clarita and her hostility toward her own mother (*Pa*), Larry's troubled relationship with his family (*Me*), and Josemar's confusion with regard to both his parents (*Sac*) demonstrate this. Behind the narratives is a series of cultural references that echo and confirm the point. In *Pubis angelical*, for example, the tragic fate of the heroine of *Lucia di Lammermoor* is caused and hastened by her kinsmen. That these are powerful and domineering men, melodramatic versions of Alejandro, whose entry into Ana's life coincided with the performance of this opera at the Teatro Colón, serves to demythify the concept of the superior man, but sentimental views of the family as haven and solace will also be undermined by knowledge of the plot. This adds to the aware reader's misgivings regarding the equation of Ana's return to her family with a happy ending. Even so, indications of the strength of family ties are interwoven with those of betrayal, and there is no clear authorial message.

Betrayal within families takes several forms, one of the most important being the outcome of generational incompatibility, a topic elaborated on in the relationship between Ramírez and Larry in *Maldición eterna a quien lea estas páginas*. Parental values are challenged and both generations regard the attitude of the other as treacherous. A further aspect of Leo's identification with Siegfried (*BAA*), which has already furnished several insights into his condition, is relevant here. If we accept Freud's association of the superego and paternal law, it could be argued that Leo's irregular upbringing has contributed greatly to his split personality, with desire and social morality/*logos*/the

law eternally in conflict. His father was always absent, and with him
the element of paternal love; what he symbolized was ever-present.
Leo was betrayed by his family and became a Siegfried, whose essentially iconoclastic autonomy and compulsive need for freedom are incompatible with love. There was, it seems, no alternative.

Individuals betray each other, and whatever they see as a reposi-
tory of beauty betrays them in its turn. Ana's daughter, Clarita (whose
name may possibly be significant[18]), appears to sense the complexity
of the issue when she is less than enthusiastic about the facile attraction of Tchaikovsky's *Nutcracker* and *The Sleeping Beauty* (*Pa* 92). In
spite of her tender years and lack of experience, she is taken with the
sombre and distressing *Giselle*, which is permeated by treachery. This
could be read as a hint that the new generation is less blind, more
demythifying, than its predecessors, but there is no suggestion from
the author that this new consciousness is totally desirable.

DISILLUSION

The consequence of betrayal should be chronic disillusion, even
despair. Nevertheless, Puig's characters manage to conserve some sort
of vision of the future. In *La traición de Rita Hayworth*, the adolescent
Toto finds a way of living with himself and coping with a society
whose *macho* standards are so alien to him: "Yo soy fuerte, más fuerte
que un bruto, porque pienso" [I'm strong, stronger than any stupid
lout, because I think], he says (*RH* 282). Then, although both Nené (*Bp*)
and Molina (*Ebma*) ultimately die, they too could be said to have
discovered a tolerable *modus vivendi* before this happens: Nené living
in the past, Molina concentrating on "cosas lindas" [beautiful things]
in order not to go insane (*Ebma* 85),[19] and then dedicating himself
body and soul to sacrificial love. Even Gladys decides against killing
herself (*BAA*); Ana (*Pa*) returns home to her mother and daughter and
is concerned for the future of her country; Larry (*Me*) is able to

---

18 Connotations of clearsightedness should not be ignored. Cf. Isabel Allende's
    novel, *La casa de los espíritus* (Barcelona: Plaza y Janés, 1982), in which the
    character named Clara is depicted as clairvoyant.

19 As Luci says in *Cae la noche tropical*, "La vida te enseña que hay que confor-
    marse con las cosas buenas mientras duran, y no sufrir cuando terminan" [Life
    teaches you to accept good things as long as you have them, and not to suffer
    when they're gone] (*Cnt* 139).

summon up enough enthusiasm for life to make some sort of fresh start; and the resilient Josemar (*Sac*), though alone, poverty-stricken, and possibly unhinged, survives by means of a false self-image and distorted memories. Indeed, many commentators are convinced that in the final analysis everything turns out well for them all. Stephanie Merrim, for example, makes the—to me—astonishing claim that all the novels have "trite resolutions," "pat solutions," and "MGM happy endings,"[20] a view that is accepted and elaborated on by Elías Miguel Muñoz,[21] while Robert Alter, in a discussion of *The Buenos Aires Affair*, considers that there is "a final possibility of hope for Gladys," an opinion that a close reading of the last pages of the book hardly supports, unless "hope" is taken to indicate survival.[22] The consensus of critical opinion also sees Ana's transformation at the end of *Pubis angelical* as a moment of inspiring and promising liberation, ignoring the conditioning of her previous life, as well as what Puig himself has said about the difficulty of adopting new roles. What appear to some to be happy endings are, in fact, instances of man's ability to survive in the face of all the odds, an authorial tribute to human resilience. There is never any question of trite resolutions.

The reader's awareness of potentially disillusioning events and experiences is reinforced by apparently arbitrary background references. That Nené's marriage (*Bp*) and her move to the capital are far from being the fulfilment of her romantically ambitious dreams is underlined when she and her dull new husband go to see the revue *Goodbye obelisco* (*Bp* 150). The obvious phallic connotations of the title suggest disappointment with the reality of sex, which she had previously seen through rose-colored spectacles, and this is, perhaps, confirmed by the information that the "chistes verdes" [blue jokes] in the show embarrassed her. At the same time it indicates that Buenos Aires itself (with its renowned obelisk) has let her down, as it was bound to

---

20 Stephanie Merrim, "For a New (Psychological) Novel in the Works of Manuel Puig," *Novel: A Forum on Fiction* 17.2 (1984): 141–57 (154).

21 Muñoz, *El discurso utópico*, 139.

22 Robert Alter, "Mimesis and the Motive for Fiction," *Tri-Quarterly* 42 (1978): 228–49 (248). Alter's judgment is more acceptable than that of Stephanie Merrim, since he refers to Gladys's ultimately finding the "courage to try to live her life again." However, given her conditioning and her age, there are few grounds for any hope of happiness.

do.[23] New places do not necessarily make for new lives, even though a film referred to in *La traición de Rita Hayworth* seems to confirm the validity of the belief that "la vie est ailleurs" [life is elsewhere], which prevails among the inhabitants of Coronel Vallejos. The film is *A La Habana me voy* (*Weekend in Havana*, with Alice Faye, John Wayne, and Carmen Miranda, dir. William Le Baron, 1941), in which an ordinary shopgirl—just like Nené in *Boquitas pintadas*—finds glamor and romance in an exotic setting. Toto is another who is obliged to repudiate his earlier illusions when he is thrust into the real world; as an adolescent he expresses contempt for Romanticism and deplores Herminia's fascination with the music of Chopin, Brahms, and Liszt (*RH* 269). He also confirms what his cousin Teté has already suggested: that he has no time at all for the consolatory notion of a loving God. The (invented) French film that he recounts to Herminia, in which an omnipotent medieval lord debilitates, tempts, and destroys the children in his care (including his own son), underlines his disenchantment with religion, and also indicates his resentful love-hate relationship with his attractive schoolmate Adhemar (who, as René Alberto Campos has observed, both provokes and denies desire[24]) and with his elusive father. In spite of all this, he survives.

So many of the cultural allusions deal with promises that it would be unwise to trust, like the false dawns of the subterranean isolation hospital in *Pubis angelical* (263),[25] the new day lying in wait for Leo in the song he mentions to his psychiatrist (*BAA* 141),[26] and the new life suggested by Herminia's spirited performance of Beethoven's *La Aurora* [Dawn],[27] after she has evicted the cynical Toto (*RH* 286). Included among the references that point in the same direction are many that we have already considered in other contexts (for example, we know—but they do not—that the members of the *Kanal* resistance

---

23 See chapter 2 of my *The Necessary Dream*. Nené's earlier hopes are also recalled by the obelisk's solar, ascendant symbolism. See Cirlot, *Diccionario*, 347. It is interesting—and an indication of the author's skill—that this reference, like so many in the novels, is authentic: there actually was a revue called *Goodbye obelisco* at the Teatro Maipo at the time.

24 Campos, *Espejos*, 107.

25 LKJS claims to live in the Avenida de la Aurora Borealis (*Pa* 205), indicating another false dawn.

26 This is obviously "Beyond the Blue Horizon."

27 As far as I can discover, there is no work by Beethoven with this title.

group will not achieve freedom, even if they escape from their living tomb), and it would be tiresome to rehearse the countless stories of thwarted longings for eternal ecstasy in the field of love. Yet the characters persevere, both men and women, though it is only the women (and those who possess "feminine" characteristics, such as Toto and Molina) who are able to do so without harming others.

THE REDUCTION OF MAN

Some of the tribulations that affect both sexes arise out of social value systems, such as the patriarchy and its offshoot, *machismo*, but others are ineluctable features of the human condition, and as such are impervious to social change. Lying behind the impossible choices typical of all the novels is the most basic of all: whether to attempt to change what can be changed or to accept the status quo. The choice is not as obvious as it might seem; Puig almost certainly suspects that certain known evils can all too easily be replaced by something equally undesirable.

The narratives not only demonstrate that injustice is both cosmic *and* social, but also show how experience obliges individuals to accommodate to reality. What clearly holds special interest for the author is the variation between traditional male and female reactions to disappointment and humiliation, and how the response of women is directed less toward the recovery of their own independent dynamism than toward adaptation to male positions. Both sexes have recourse to survival tactics, but, traditionally, women feel that they will benefit in proportion to the degree of their partner's self-esteem.

On a social level, therefore, the reduction of men affects both sexes, and men are reduced when their sexual, financial, social, or intellectual self-image is damaged. Since in a patriarchal society this is unjustifiably grandiose, the resulting fall is painful indeed, and the male struggle to regain at least the appearance of powerful superiority will be equally distressing for caring women.

It is not difficult to think of narrative instances of humiliated men and their *macho* responses. In the first novel, for example, Toto's father, Berto, judges himself diminished on all four fronts. He is no longer the ladykiller he once was (*RH* 25, 26, 29); his plan to make a fortune has failed, and he resents his wife's working (*RH* 16) (there is even some doubt as to his ability to afford furniture for their rented house [*RH* 29]); his social impotence is demonstrated when he attacks Mita's employer (*RH* 24, 29); and his wife's professional qualification and her family's attempts to find him a job suggest that he is her intellectual and social inferior. His bitter resentment, expressed in the letter to his brother that was never mailed, results in chronic bad temper and bouts of violence that affect everyone in his immediate vicinity—particularly, of course, his wife, who often weeps when she is alone. Then, in *Boquitas pintadas*, Juan Carlos's sexual promiscuity may be seen as the only means available to him of acquiring a sense of power: he has been cheated out of an inheritance, has no social standing, and is barely literate. When his career as a Don Juan is terminated by illness, there is nothing left for him except death. In *Sangre de amor correspondido*, because Josemar's wealthy father has never acknowledged him, he finds himself in a similar position, and survives by means of the pretence that he is independent, powerful, and sexually ruthless.

It is, or has been, generally accepted that men never question their right to power, and one of the questions that exercises Puig is why this should be so. If we turn to the field of non-psychoanalytic psychology, it is easy to discern a certain sympathy with cognitive–developmental theory, which argues that children (who are originally unaware of sexual difference in Freud's view) actually learn patterns of behavior and thought based on gender. The system, according to Kohlberg, persists from generation to generation because it provides children with protection against insecurity about their gender identity.[28] The theory can be applied to both sexes, but for boys the characteristics acquired by means of observational learning find their most extreme manifestations in *machismo*, which reflects and conserves a sense of superiority. Contemporary studies point out that television is the strongest influence on gender stereotypes in young minds, but the influence of culture on the perception of gender identity has been with us since culture began.

As we have already noted, Puig uses the myth of the fall of Icarus to reflect the failure of Gladys's male schoolmate to establish his superiority by winning a sculpture competition (*BAA*). The boy's subsequent reaction to his rival also invites investigation, since this is gender-oriented; like the eponymous incredible shrinking man of the film recounted by Larry (*Me*), it is his masculinity that has been impugned. Gladys had been almost sure that "lograría el amor del

---

28 L. Kohlberg, "A Cognitive-Developmental Analysis of Children's Sex-Role Concepts and Attitudes," in *The Development of Sex Differences*, ed. E.E. Maccoby (Stanford: Stanford UP, 1966).

joven" [she would win the young man's love] but, in the event, he ignores her and is "desdeñoso" [disdainful] toward her (*BAA* 37, 38). His hurtful defense/power stratagem is to withhold love. The original Icarus legend can be interpreted in keeping with cognitive–developmental principles, for although it was Icarus's *folie des grandeurs* that provoked his downfall, the blame for his circumstances can be laid at the feet of his father, Daedalus. (Indeed, in one version of the myth, Daedalus is included among the countless fathers who actually sacrifice their sons.[29])

When Nené and her husband are on their honeymoon, they go to see a performance of the play *Con las alas rotas* [With Broken Wings] (*Bp* 151),[30] a title that could be said to apply to everyone. However, the reaction of Puig's women characters to "reduction," though also involving stereotypical behavior and attitudes, is more complex. They continue to espouse their betrayed illusions with all their strength, even—as in the case of Choli (*RH*)—to the point of absurdity; they renounce their autonomy, in Simone de Beauvoir's phrase,[31] observing and pandering to male values. The female approach is more subtle than that of the male. No one disputes that men are rewarded for *macho* behavior but it is less apparent that women at least hope to benefit from passivity. Ultimately, perhaps, there is little to choose between the levels of male and female egocentricity, but even if that premise is accepted, Puig, at least, was in no doubt as to the higher moral and social value of what are seen as "feminine" qualities, which, surprisingly, come increasingly to the fore when it might be reasonable to suppose that disillusion would result in subversiveness.

It was Josef Breuer, an early colleague of Freud's, who attributed female neurosis to the incompatibility between the circumstances of

---

29 See Robert Graves, *The White Goddess: A Historical Grammar of Poetic Myth* (London: Faber, 1961) 127–28.

30 This melodrama was one of the actress Camila Quiroga's greatest triumphs, according to Mecha Ortiz, who herself played the leading role in the later film version (1938). *Mecha Ortiz*, 123. It is, perhaps, significant that the protagonist was a woman.

31 Simone de Beauvoir, *The Second Sex*, trans. H.M. Parshley (1949; Harmondsworth: Penguin, 1972) 307. Simone de Beauvoir was also responsible for the well-known judgment that "one is not born, but rather becomes, a woman" (295).

women's daily lives and their daydreams.[32] These daydreams were, of course, repressed, and therapy consisted of hypnosis (under Breuer) and "free association" (with Freud). Puig's female characters are different, since it is the pedestrian monotony of daily life that is repressed, and they actually survive by means of daydreams. (It is significant that in *Boquitas pintadas* Nené's abandonment of illusion coincides with her death.) Unlike Freud and Breuer's hysterical patients, their daydreams do not challenge established social norms, but are actually conditioned by them. They fall into two principal areas, a desire for asexual—even courtly—love, and masochism, and both of these are illuminated by cultural references.

Puig's women (including Toto and Molina) often display an aversion to sex itself, implying that a *pubis angelical* would eradicate all the griefs of this world. However, it is not a question of renouncing *sexuality*; they long to be continuously admired, desired, and wooed by a protective, gentle, "feminized" man. As Maria Laplace observes, eternal courtship would guarantee the prolongation of passion and desire and "the hegemonic placement of woman in the family [would be] subverted."[33] The image of the romantic hero is also born of female self-interest, for he is caring and admiring, and "capable of nurturing the heroine." Just like Mabel's vision of Robert Taylor or Tyrone Power (*Bp*), this kind of desire "focuses on the lovers' faces and, in particular, the eyes and mouth. The gaze, the kiss, the voice, become the locus of eroticism,"[34] and, paradoxically—given the woman's passivity—possession and domination are deferred. Weakness may therefore be seen as fundamentally manipulative, and the taste for sexless love stories (such as *Paul et Virginie* and the Rogers and Astaire musicals) among the women of Coronel Vallejos should not surprise us.

It is a short step from this approach to female masochism—not the masochistic perversion of the sexologists, but Erich Fromm's masochistic *character*: "pain and suffering are not what [s]he wants, pain and suffering are the price [s]he pays for an aim which [s]he compulsively

---

32 Josef Breuer, with Sigmund Freud, "Studies on Hysteria," *SE* 2 (1895).

33 Laplace, "Producing and Consuming," 161.

34 Laplace, "Producing and Consuming," 159.

tries to attain."[35] Because "masochistic phenomena . . . are looked upon as expressions of love,"[36] this is a comfortable attitude for women, but it is generally thought that both masochism and sadism co-exist within the same individual, and that both of them are manifestations of a craving for power. Again, there seems little to choose between the motives of men and women, unless we accept Fromm's view that "power" can mean both potency and domination. It is the latter that is striven after by *macho* men, and this is a "perversion of potency," for potency is the ability "to realise . . . potentialities on the basis of freedom and integrity of [the] self."[37]

Whatever their fundamental motivation, and whatever Puig's attitude toward this may be, the allusions to sacrificial heroines in books, plays, films, and operas indicate the extent of their fascination for his women characters. Both *El capitán herido* [The Wounded Captain] and *La promesa olvidada* [The Broken Promise], the radio soap-operas that are so popular with Mabel and Nené (*Bp* 200), portray masochistic, caring women and deceitful men, as do so many of the books, operas, and films referred to throughout the texts—*Marianela, Tannhäuser, La Fanciulla del West, Rigoletto, The Great Waltz, The Great Ziegfeld,* and *Intermezzo,* to name but a few. The tragic element in the masochistic stratagem (for stratagem it surely is), indirectly indicated by means of cultural allusions, is women's assumption that further "reduction" is inevitable. The descent into alcoholism of the inconsolable heroine of *I'll Cry Tomorrow,* which acts as a counterpoint to Gladys's doomed relationship with Leo (*BAA*), is but one instance of the unthinking complaisance of audiences.

It is all too easy to attribute condemnatory motives to Puig as he contrasts the lust for power traditionally found in men with women's apparently perverse masochism. Nevertheless, in conversation he often referred to the suffering of men as they attempted to live up to the demands of *machismo.* He felt that the twin aims of both sexes in their struggle against oppression are survival and happiness. Only their stratagems vary, and it is the resilience of both sexes as they adapt to harsh reality that fascinated the author.

---

35 Fromm, *The Fear of Freedom* (1942; London: Routledge, 1961) 133. For a more detailed examination of Gladys's masochism in *The Buenos Aires Affair,* see my *The Necessary Dream.*

36 Fromm, *The Fear of Freedom,* 138.

37 Fromm, *The Fear of Freedom,* 140, 139.

VII

Destiny

DETERMINISM

IT IS INCONTROVERTIBLE that there is a strong vein of determinism in all the novels, but because culture both echoes and perpetuates attitudes, this is not cultural determinism, as Stephanie Merrim claims, nor is it to be deplored, as she suggests—unless it is the human predicament itself (as Puig sees it) that merits this reaction.[1] In his view, the psyche *is* determined, but by a variety of forces. Some are indeed aspects of social and cultural conditioning—emanating from the so-called culture industry—but others are not; in any case, there is little doubt that he has no faith in the concept of "the free man." For him there is no end to our complexity. First of all, it is virtually impossible to know which human traits are constitutional (determined) and which are accidental (conditioned). These are often mutually incompatible, and their co-existence gives rise to a necessity for painful choices. Then, even if it were possible to discern suitable areas of modification, there is no guarantee that change would mean unconditional improvement. Courage, if not foolhardiness, is necessary to alter a world view and a lifestyle.

---

1 "Unfortunately a dark note of cultural determinism underlines Puig's pop works, and unites all of his novels under its sign." Merrim claims that his characters "have been rendered 'zombies' by the culture that significantly determines their way of thinking" and that there is no question of seeing Puig as a "sophisticated" writer. "For a New (Psychological) Novel," 156–57.

One constitutional circumstance that is constantly in evidence in the texts is the relationship with the father. Puig once went as far as to say that the key to *La traición de Rita Hayworth* is Berto's absence,[2] and the fact that Leo's father plays no part in his early life is a vital clue to any interpretation of *The Buenos Aires Affair*. Ramírez provides a paternal image for Larry in *Maldición eterna a quien lea estas páginas*, and many of Josemar's problems in *Sangre de amor correspondido* stem from his desire to be accepted by his true father. It is also more than likely that Ana's lifelong search for a superior man in *Pubis angelical* is based on the need for a substitute for her late father. There are, in fact, countless paternal substitutes throughout the texts, including Peronism, the prison authorities in *El beso de la mujer araña*—and Valentín himself, if we bear in mind that Navaho mythology includes a Spider Woman who can control the movements of the sun with her web.[3] Then there are numerous messianic/paternal lovers: the *Actriz*'s "Él" (*Pa*), Gladys's Leo (*BAA*) (with the solar connotations of his name), and Juan Carlos (*Bp*), whose initials may not be fortuitous.

Given Puig's interest in Freudian theory, it is perhaps worth recalling Freud's own words:

> The psychology of individual human beings . . . teaches us with quite special insistence that the god of each of them is formed in the likeness of his father, that his personal relation to God depends on his relation to his father in the flesh and oscillates and changes along with that relation, and that at bottom, God is nothing other than an exalted father.[4]

What Joseph Campbell calls "the ogre aspect of the father"[5] can therefore be projected onto God, who is then envisaged as wrathful and cruel,[6] but the God behind Puig's religious determinism is, rather, neglectful and uncaring. It is not that He does not exist (Toto's allegorical film story of the medieval lord proves this), but, like the earthly

---

2 Sosnowski, "Entrevista," 72.

3 See Campbell, *The Hero with a Thousand Faces*, 71.

4 Freud, "Totem and Taboo," *SE* 13 (1912–13).

5 Campbell, *The Hero with a Thousand Faces*, 129.

6 For example, in Jonathan Edwards, *Sinners in the Hands of an Angry God* (Boston, 1742).

fathers of the narratives, He is absent. The obsessive father-complexes in those characters who are conscious of how their lives have been shaped, even blighted, by a less than perfect relationship with their fathers—Josemar (*Sac*) is the most striking example—are not all that far removed from confused and resentful attitudes toward God, such as that of Larry (*Me*), or from ambivalence in the face of authority. Freud's view of generational, and therefore religious, determinism is well summarized by Jung, who refers to his view of "wicked paternal authority" and then goes on:

> The motif of the Gnostic Yahweh and Creator-God reappeared in the Freudian myth of the primal father and the gloomy superego deriving from that father. . . . He became a daimon who created a world of disappointments, illusions and suffering.[7]

Disappointments, illusions, and suffering are everyday experiences for Puig's characters, and there is no avoiding these, for any savior and protector, be he a father, a superior man, or God Himself, can be counted on to betray simple-minded human ideals.

A close reading of a particular section of Puig's largely autobiographical first novel provides evidence of the link between the fatalism of the relationship with the father and a sense of occult, hostile destiny. This is the point at which Toto has been reprimanded by Berto, and is thinking about the admirable qualities of Shirley Temple, who, in *The Little Colonel*, is so good that she wins the love of her "abuelo malo" [wicked grandfather]. "Yo voy a ser bueno como la Shirley" [I'm going to be good like Shirley], Toto vows (*RH* 44–46). Running through this stream-of-consciousness chapter is an invented tale in which Toto is metamorphosed into first a bird, then a little girl, and finally a fish, in his attempt to escape from a gypsy and rescue Shirley Temple. As René Alberto Campos has noted, "el motivo básico que desencadena toda esta proyección de la fantasía es el temor a la figura del padre. Berto [se convierte] en el abuelo malo de Shirley, en el gitano y en el dueño del pececito . . ." [The basic motivation for this projection is fear of the father. Berto (is converted) into Shirley's wicked grandfather, the gypsy, and the owner of the fish . . .].[8] The

---

7 C.G. Jung, *Memories, Dreams, Reflections*, rec. and ed. Anniela Jaffé, trans. Richard and Clara Winston (1961; London: Fontana, 1983) 227.

8 Campos, *Espejos*, 50.

presence of a *pececito* needs no explanation, since Toto has just seen an underwater documentary film, but the myth of the terrifying gypsy ogre who abducts children and covers them with coal dust invites investigation. The traditional association of gypsies with clairvoyant powers, and therefore predestination, is underlined by the image of coal, which connotes hidden energy and a nature which, though as yet unknown, already exists and is immutable.[9] Toto is killing two birds with one stone in this story: he is proving his virtue and valor, with the aim of placating the evil side of his father, but at the same time he is avoiding a sinister manifestation of destiny.

A fatalistic viewpoint is frequently discernible in the texts, and there are many quotations of titles that also point to predestination. One of the films being shown in Buenos Aires during the military régime is *Nacidos el unto para el otro* (*Made for Each Other*, with Renée Taylor and Joseph Bologna, dir. Robert B. Bean, 1971) (*Pa* 165): this suggests that Ana's relationship with Pozzi, who bears a close resemblance to the leading actor, was preordained. Then there is the film *Fatalidad* [Fate] (*BAA*, epigraph to chapter 13); the original English title was *Dishonored* (with Marlene Dietrich and Victor McLaglen, dir. Josef von Sternberg, 1931), but the dialogue that is reproduced stresses the ineluctable nature of what has happened as well as the equally unappealing options that this heroine, like Gladys herself, has to confront. The title of the Nazi propaganda film in *El beso de la mujer araña* is, of course, *Destino* [Destiny]; Leni, like Molina, is the pawn of fate. Many fictional works that have already been considered in other contexts focus on inexorable disaster (fate—*Fatum*—is always hostile). *Cat People* (*Ebma*), together with its medieval prototype story, is particularly relevant. People are born to follow certain paths: ". . . yo nací . . . con la luna de plata, / y nací . . . con alma de pirata . . ." [. . . I was born . . . under the silver moon, / and I was born . . . with the soul of a pirate . . .], sings the *Actriz* (*Pa* 137); and in the Mario Clavel bolero "Mi carta" [My Letter] (*Ebma* 137–42), which an initially scornful Valentín eventually agrees is "really quite good" (*Ebma* 141), we find lines that echo the situation of all doomed lovers ("aunque la vida no nos una nunca, / Y estemos—porque es preciso—siempre separados . . ." [Even if life never unites us, / And—because there is

---

9 Jean Chevalier and Alain Gheerbrant, *Dictionnaire des Symboles* (Paris: Robert Laffont and Éditions Jupiter, 1982) 211.

no option—we are apart for ever . . .]), which are followed by a defiant declaration of eternal fidelity, all that is possible in the circumstances.

Even though the author would be unlikely to defend the wilder manifestations of vital determinism, there is much to suggest that he suspects that many psychological traits are innate and immutable. This attitude is represented and emphasized in the texts by allusions to fiction. That some of these signifiers have been judged aesthetically worthless does not diminish what is signified. The popular manifestation of determinism, which is even more susceptible to condemnation, is astrology, and this comes into its own in *Maldición eterna a quien lea estas páginas*. Indeed, without recourse to astrological symbology, many of the images, and some of the information we are given, would be entirely inexplicable.[10] For example, Larry, who is a Pisces subject, teases Ramírez by recounting a bizarre, recurring dream he has had about fish (*Me* 59–60), and this appears to be totally redundant. The nurse's sign is Virgo—caring, devoted to others, and attracted to those born under Pisces, but like all Puig's nurses also a maternal figure, since Virgo is linked to Isis, who is both the goddess of medicine and the Divine Mother. One of the few things that the amnesiac Ramírez has not forgotten is that his birth sign is Capricorn. A pattern emerges, for Capricorn is a goat with a fish tail: Larry, his surrogate son, is part of him. Then, Ramírez has travelled north (from Argentina to New York), which is a journey toward essence: Capricorn is a cardinal sign representing winter, and the old man is travelling toward death, after which his surrogate son will replace him in the world. It may not be arbitrary that this happens on 2 February, traditionally the date of the presentation in the temple, which signified Christ's emancipation from His earthly parents. Since, in this novel, the "father" does not in the end devour the "son" (as Larry had feared he would), it is spirit, not matter that survives. Can it be coincidence that the astrological Great Year, which represents the triumph of the spirit, is also known as the Piscean Age? Yet again, there is authorial ambivalence regarding this topic. The astrological pattern is very consciously elaborated, and it is another area in which the reader's attention is drawn to the conflict between what is ineluctable and what may be modified. As Michel Gauquelin says:

---

10 For an investigation of the astrological element in this novel, see my *The Necessary Dream*.

> If the notion still persists today that the secret of our fate resides in the movement of the stars, it is because it corresponds to something deep and lasting in the minds of men, something akin to the need to eat, fight, or make love. It is a naïve and subjective way of understanding the world through oneself.[11]

And he offers a theory that might be acceptable to some:

> A child's organism cannot be abruptly modified at birth by planetary influences; agreed. But why should it not happen the other way about: the child might have a predisposition to come into the world under certain cosmic conditions which corresponded to his biological constitution. In a way, the child would be waiting for the right time to be born, and this moment would merely be an indication of his biological make-up. The position of the planet would make no difference to the child's constitution. And it would be this constitution—the biological temperament inherited from its parents—which alone would give its life a specific direction, pushing it, for instance, into a particular profession. The star would therefore not play any part in predetermining the future.

He goes on to admit that astronomers and biologists will find the hypothesis improbable,[12] but it contributes to a serious assessment of the role of astrology in Puig. It holds, after all, that the future can be predicted only by weighing up the past, and this is made up of attitudes, drives, actions, and events that are closely dependent on what Gauquelin calls the biological makeup of the individual. "Los astros no determinan lo que es el individuo, sino que lo expresan" [the stars do not determine the individual, they express what he is], claims André Barbault.[13] However, even if this dictum is accepted, it does not account for imposed values or socially created desires. *Sapiens dominabitur astris*, according to St. Thomas Aquinas, and Schiller once assured an acquaintance: "In deiner Brust sind deine Schicksals Sterne" [The stars of your destiny are located in your own heart]. It may be that the

11 Michel Gauquelin, *Astrology and Science*, trans. James Hughes (1966; London: Granada, 1972) 32.

12 Gauquelin, *Astrology and Science*, 156.

13 André Barbault, *Del psicoanálisis a la astrología* (Buenos Aires: Editorial Dédalo, 1975) 26. Translation of *De la Psychanalyse à l'astrologie* (Paris: Éditions du Seuil, 1961).

most of us are ambivalent on this subject: when decisions have to be made, few people indulge in total passivity. Even if humans are not free the imagination can be, and individual defense stratagems vary.

Yet there is a sense in the novels of a common destiny. One of the sources of this is a certain amount of repetition, with echoes and parallels in the names of the characters. Raquel Linenberg-Fressard has done some interesting work in this field, investigating "dans quelle mesure les noms de personnage parviennent à mimer leur signifié narratif" [how far the characters' names reflect their narrative function].[14] This is indeed a fruitful task, since without exception all the names are the result of amendments to the first drafts of the novels. Because the characters are to a greater or lesser extent based on real people—the opening chapter of *La traición de Rita Hayworth*, for example, was originally made up of the thoughts of the author's aunt, Larry (*Me*) was a New York friend, and Josemar (*Sac*) a Rio de Janeiro workman—virtually all the changes were originally made in order to avoid recognition of the real-life model, and the fictional names were chosen very carefully indeed. They can all be classified by means of the phrase that Raquel Linenberg-Fressard uses for only some of them: "noms pleinement motivés" [names full of significance]. It is amusing to tease out the implications of the author's choices, especially as they are often highly ironic. One example, from *La traición de Rita Hayworth*, is the discovery that the relatives of the (invented) Argentine film actor Carlos Palau[15] live in a *conventillo* [slum tenement] (*RH* 11), since in Catalan *palau* means "palace."

Raquel Linenberg-Fressard's two articles not only provide us with insights of this sort, but also draw our attention to the fact that the characters themselves are conscious of both the morphological and semantic import of other people's names.[16] Although some of her

---

14 Raquel Linenberg-Fressard, "Les noms de personnage dans *La traición de Rita Hayworth*, de Manuel Puig," *Les Langues Néo-Latines* 3.254 (1985): 81–93 (81). See also "La motivation des noms de personnage dans *Pubis angelical* de Manuel Puig," *Imprévue* 1 (1966): 99–109.

15 The character is, in fact, based on a real Argentine actor.

16 For example, Esther (*RH*) writes in her diary: "Héctor.... ¿ .. eres silencioso como la primera letra de tu nombre?" [Héctor, are you silent like the first letter of your name?] (*RH* 225). In *Pubis angelical* Ana and Pozzi discuss the implications of Alejandro's name. In the first draft of this novel, Ana compares the names of her husband and her lover: "Fito con fi de finalidad," [Fito with fi as

interpretations are debatable, especially regarding *Pubis angelical*,[17] she is gratifyingly aware of what she calls a "jeu des reflets" [specular game];[18] it is this, rather than semantics, that concerns us in the present context. Reflections are found among the characters and in the cultural figures that influence and reflect these. Sometimes parallels exist within the same novel, but it is only when the texts are considered as a whole that it becomes clear that onomastic connections are not arbitrary. Furthermore, it is not just a question of names, but also of descriptive tags. For example, the phrase "the most beautiful woman in the world" is used several times by Ana (*Pa*) in her Hedy Lamarr projection (the Austrian actress was often thus labelled), and with Puig's unequalled knowledge of the cinema, it is likely that one of the implications of the *locas'* choice of Gina (Lollobrigida) as one of their models (*Ebma*) had something to do with the fact that one of this actress's best-known films was *La Donna Più Bella del Mondo* (dir. Robert Z. Leonard, 1955).

Mankind's common destiny is not the only thing suggested by the duplication of names; it also indicates the alternative possibilities that are theoretically open to each character. At times these are based on knowledge of the stereotypes that the names evoke, while in other cases it is their semantic value that is relevant. What is always striking is that, yet again, the options presented constitute impossible choices, and that the world is so often being viewed from within the psyche of a character. A distressing aspect of this dualistic situation is that both the cultural stereotype suggested by a name and the concept evoked by its meaning can lead to betrayal. One example of specularity within the same text is found when Toto spends his parents' siesta hour producing a poster for the film *En el viejo Chicago* (*In Old Chicago*, with Alice Faye, Tyrone Power, and Don Ameche, dir. Henry King, 1938). He concentrates on tracing the (blonde) leading actress's face (*RH* 70), and in a matter of seconds—and for obvious reasons—his thoughts

---

in final] and "Pozzi con po de poder ¿o de posesión?" [Pozzi with po as in power. Or possession?].

17 Her account of the choice of W218 and LKJS for one of Ana's projections is somewhat over-ingenious. They are actually variations on ciphers that replace the names of the protagonists of George Lucas's 1970 film, *THX 1138*, on which this section of the novel was based: in the film, the hero was THX 1138 and the heroine, LUH 3417.

18 Linenberg-Fressard, "La motivation des noms," 109.

turn to his (blonde) friend Alicita. In the cinematic context, the name Alice connotes a good–bad woman whose basic virtue eventually wins over the family of the man she loves, but Alicita is frivolous, flirtatious, and—most annoying of all—completely uninterested in Toto. Like Rita Hayworth, she is a betrayer of ideals.[19] Of course, gullibility in a child is comprehensible; that of adults is less so, until we realize that refusing to challenge generational conditioning will preclude the acquisition of maturity at any age. This is particularly true of Puig's women. When Ana (*Pa*), in her W218 projection, uses the name Dora, it may be a subconscious echo of Dorabella in Mozart's *Così fan tutte*, who—as we have seen—she inaccurately suggests is the embodiment of innocence. Conversely, her resistance to her friend Beatriz finds a parallel in the name of the *Actriz*'s Hollywood dresser, "la odiada Betsy" [the hated Betsy] (*Pa* 108). In both cases Ana reveals her failure to question mistaken *idées reçues*: that beauty can be equated with virtue and that the assertiveness of an independently minded woman is synonymous with the repellent and unchallengeable bullying that is traditionally associated with powerful men. The last thing a woman like Ana wants is to be labelled unfeminine.

A broader view of the novels and the cultural references reveals repetition of men's as well as women's names.[20] Among these are Berto/Roberto/Robert and Alberto, Alejandro, Juan, José, and Luis. Robert(o) and Albert(o) have more or less the same *macho* connotations: brilliant fame and brilliant lineage.[21] Needless to say, there is no question of the characters who bear these names (Berto [*RH*] and [Luis] Alberto Molina [*Ebma*]) living up to them.[22] However, since male role models are as polarized as those available to women, no "real" man is likely to settle for the opposite extreme. The acceptable

---

19 René Alberto Campos makes this point in *Espejos*, 58–59.

20 Even in Puig's unpublished work, names are repeated. The heroine of *La tajada* is Nélida, prefiguring Nené in *Boquitas pintadas*, and the wife of a Peronist minister is called Mariester (like the youg Peronist in *La traición de Rita Hayworth* and Leo's friend in *The Buenos Aires Affair*). In the first draft of *The Buenos Aires Affair*, the names of Clara Evelia's mother-in-law and father-in-law appear: they are María Esther and José Luis.

21 See Gutierre Tibón, *Diccionario de nombres propios*, 2nd ed. (Mexico City: Fondo de Cultura Económica, 1986).

22 Yet another Robert is Bob Giusto, one of Gladys's North American lovers (*BAA* 45 *et seq.*), who turns out to be nothing like her romantic ideal.

alternative is indicated by references to Robert Taylor and Roberto Carlos (whose sentimental songs the basically non-*macho* Josemar [*Sac*] likes), but their "feminized" image, though appealing to the women, is too gentle to be acceptable: better by far to cover up weakness with ruthlessness, like Alejandro in *Pubis angelical*. At first, given the admirable qualities of the model, the name of this character seems singularly inappropriate, but then we recall that in her *Razón de mi vida*, Eva Duarte de Perón revealed that Alexander the Great was her husband's favorite historical figure.

The frequency of common names like Juan (Juan Carlos [*Bp*], Pozzi [*Pa*], Larry [Giovanangelo], and Ramírez [*Me*]), José (Toto [*RH*], Molina [*Ebma*], Pozzi [*Pa*], Ramírez [*Me*], and Josemar [*Sac*]); and Luis (Toto and Molina) underscores the notion of human interchangeability and also contributes to what Barthes called "l'effet du réel."[23] The same is true of the numerous Marías among the female characters, even though these are often revealingly qualified. It is the shared nature of names, implying a shared destiny, that is relevant, but two examples of the way that qualification serves to reinforce and clarify themes demonstrate that nothing in Puig is fortuitous. In *Sangre de amor correspondido* Josemar fails to seduce Maria da Gloria, but has children by (Maria de) Lourdes: the former is the unattainable, heavenly Virgin, while the latter is the Virgin made flesh.[24]

According to esoteric theory, the name is an expression of an individual's horoscope,[25] and traditionally, too, it is identified with character, and therefore destiny.[26] The primitive practice of giving positive, descriptive names to the newborn was therefore a magic defense against future disaster. The motivation behind an author's choice of names for his fictional creations is often more disingenuous. With Puig they emphasize the inaccessibility of the ideal signified either by a model or by their meaning, with irony in evidence in the fact that repeated names, far from ensuring success, happiness, and glory, indicate a preordained common inability to achieve any of these.

---

23 Roland Barthes, "L'Effet du réel," *Communications* 2 (1968): 84–89.

24 Other repeated/reflected names are: Est(h)er, Clar(it)a, Ramírez, Azucena (*Sac* and *Il Trovatore*), Herminia (*RH*)/Minnie (*La Fanciulla del West*).

25 See Marc Saunier, *La Légende des symboles* (Paris: E. Sansot, 1911).

26 Cirlot, *Diccionario*, 339.

LIVING WITH DEATH

Despite what I judge to be the misconceptions of those critics who have been misled by the references to mass culture that constitute but a part of the intertext of Puig's novels, it is clear that the purpose of these is as serious as that of the allusions to High Art, and that their overall effect is equally sombre and pessimistic. All of them portray life as a series of enforced choices with little to recommend either available option. They confirm Larry's view (*Me* 153) that happiness is in short supply, underline its ephemerality, and suggest that disillusion will almost certainly ensue. They highlight predetermination, and they dwell on the only incontrovertibly preordained human circumstance: death.[27]

Commentators who have dwelt on Puig's humor and frivolity may be surprised by the frequency of death in the texts: among those who die are Mita's baby and Toto's uncle (*RH*); Juan Carlos, Pancho, and Nené (*Bp*); Gladys's father, Leo's parents, a homosexual prostitute, and Leo himself (*BAA*); Molina and Valentín (*Ebma*); and Pozzi (*Pa*), Ramírez (*Me*), and Luci (*Cnt*). The tenor of of the novels ranges from the melancholy (*Cae la noche tropical*) to the unremittingly comfortless. *Boquitas pintadas* is an example of the latter, and the tone is established immediately, since it opens with a death notice, which triggers off the action (though the term is somewhat inappropriate as almost everything has already happened). The title of *The Buenos Aires Affair* and the detective story formula that it suggests have a similar warning effect on the potential reader, for death is implicitly indicated. The threat of death is never far away in *El beso de la mujer araña*, and the same is true of *Pubis angelical*, with Ana gravely ill and Pozzi involved in insurrectional violence. It soon becomes obvious that the verbal cat-and-mouse game played by Ramírez and Larry in *Maldición eterna a quien lea estas páginas* is a struggle from which only one of the protagonists will emerge alive. Finally, the title, emphasis on the passage of time, and the age of the two protagonists of *Cae la noche tropical* all provide a sense of an ending.

---

27 As John Updike recently wrote, "[Puig's] world is a dark and harsh one, lit only by the thousand guttering candles of persistent human romanticism." "Nobody Gets Away with Everything," *The New Yorker* (25 May 1992) 84.

There are also fairly frequent discussions and observations on the subject of death on the part of the characters, with references to the void (*el vacío*) and the abyss (*el abismo*) and little hope of comfort in heaven: only anticipation of annihilation. One of the two reactions depicted is rational and resigned, and this is encapsulated in Pozzi's vision of a worthwhile death. "No me importa lo que me pase a mí, si es por algo que vale la pena" [I don't care what happens to me if it serves a useful purpose] (*Pa* 220). The other is typical of those who allow sentiment and the imagination to dictate their world view, and is therefore permeated with fear, even terror. "A mí me da miedo cada vez que me acuerdo de esa pieza que canta," confesses Molina in characteristic fashion, when describing Leni's performances in *Destino*, "porque cuando la canta está como mirando fijo en el vacío" [I'm afraid every time I recall that song she sings, because when she's singing it's as if she's gazing into the void] (*Ebma* 58).

In practice, both attitudes produce the same effect. Neither of them involves faith in the Christian heaven, so that it is the here and now that must be improved. Demystifying characters such as Valentín, Pozzi, and Larry concentrate on understanding and changing everyday life, while Gladys, Molina, Ana, and Josemar—and Toto in his early years—direct their efforts toward sweetening it with wishful illusions, which are reinforced by mention of the *type* of culture that they enjoy.

Nevertheless, Puig's choice of *specific* cultural references indicates that a consciousness of death continually sullies their daydreams. As we have seen, Molina's allusion to Sparafucile indirectly reveals that he too is a potential killer, and it is followed by another that confirms this, one that links predestination and death and again points to the sinister image of gypsies (enemies of order and harmony and advocates of the hegemony of the essential). This is the moment when he tells Valentín that his real name is Carmen, "la de Bizet" (Bizet's *Carmen* [1875]) (*Ebma* 72). Molina is speaking of his devotion to the unattainable heterosexual waiter, Gabriel, so that the reference to Mérimée's irresistible *femme fatale* is singularly inappropriate unless it is seen as reflecting Molina's basic awareness of the ineluctable link between death and uncontrollable sexuality. In the opera, as in this novel, both protagonists die.

Even the most naïvely optimistic characters are inconveniently invaded by a consciousness of mortality. One of these is Herminia (*RH*), who, at thirty-five, still cherishes a spark of hope for future happiness. In the course of her ruminations, she mentions a Danish philosopher, Gustav Hansen (*RH* 268–69), whose theories posit "la inmensidad de lo material en contraposición a la significancia de lo espiritual" [the immensity of the material compared with the spiritual]. Like the other Dane referred to by the author, Dr. Anneli Taube (*Ebma*), there is no such authority as Gustav Hansen, so that it is clear that the views attributed to him are expressed solely to emphasize Herminia's determination to cling to spiritual values in an attempt to enrich her life. "En no todos los casos tiene razón" [He's not always right], she asserts (*RH* 269). Conversely, the cold despair of those who reject all faith in life is reflected in works of art whose essence is nihilistic and bitter, such as *tachiste* painting and the works of Rouault in the case of Leo (*BAA*), and the writings of Camus and Sartre, which are associated with Larry (*Me*).

Awareness of death on the part of the characters may, in fact, be a key to all the novels. Those who undertake a quest for romantic love, whatever the cost, indicate a defiant, even perverse, struggle for survival and happiness, while clearsighted activists, who scorn the delusions of others, courageously indulge in what Joseph Campbell refers to as "open-eyed observation of the sickeningly broken figurations that abound before us, around us, and within." For these modern heroes "there is no make-believe . . . to alleviate the bitter majesty, but only utter darkness, the void of unfulfilment, to receive and eat back the lives that have been tossed forth from the womb only to fail,"[28] and they suggest that there is nothing at all to be said for romantic wishful thinking and self-deception ("You just go on lying to yourself and deceiving yourself," says Pozzi to Ana after revealing to her that she is terminally ill [*Pa* 223]). Puig understands, condones, and even admires this attitude, for—in Campbell's words—although faith in a happy ending means that "the objective world remains what it was, but because of a shift of emphasis within the subject, is beheld as though transformed. . . . The wild and careless, inexhaustible joy of life [is] invincible."[29]

---

28 Campbell, *The Hero with a Thousand Faces*, 27.

29 Campbell, *The Hero with a Thousand Faces*, 28.

VIII

Conclusion

WHEN I SPENT THE SUMMER of 1987 consulting the notes for the seven novels that Manuel Puig had then published (*Cae la noche tropical* was to appear in 1988[1]), together with the first drafts of these, my suspicion that the cultural references had been late additions was confirmed. Further investigation revealed that these references had been very thoroughly researched, or in some cases—and this seemed to me to be equally significant—had been invented by the author after consideration of the possible effect of their presence within the texts. The mention of the work of Gustav Hansen in *La traición de Rita Hayworth* and the inclusion of the theories of Dr. Anneli Taube in the otherwise accurately summarized psychological footnotes to *El beso de la mujer araña* are the most striking examples of the creation of spurious, but apparently authoritative, sources for ideas that the author himself wanted to air. These discoveries meant that there could no longer be any doubt as to the significance of the intertextual allusions

---

1 An interesting aspect of the last novel is that the passage of time has reduced the impact of culture on the protagonists. Nidia and Luci find it difficult to remember the names of artists they once admired (*Cnt* 33), which movie they saw (*Cnt* 45), and an excursion they once made to Brontë country (*Cnt* 32).

in any attempt to understand and interpret textual intent.[2] Moreover, I felt that their very existence constituted evidence of the author's craftsmanship, which some commentators had steadfastly failed to recognize.[3]

Of course, it came as no surprise when I found that the aspects of the mass media that are so frequently alluded to in the novels had been painstakingly researched: "the culture industry" has always been a favorite topic with Puig's critics and it was this area of focus, together with the utilization of language that reproduces the commonplaces of River Plate speech, that provoked critical shock and scorn in the early days. However, research confirmed my original view that many of those who were sympathetic to Puig had misrepresented his work when they claimed that since the characters most imbued with the style, values, and ideology of this largely alien, and certainly alienating, culture are undeniably foolish, his attitude toward this was totally negative and that he was wholeheartedly positing sensible, progressive alternatives. They supposed that it would be impossible to condone the pursuit of ideals that are clearly unattainable, and that in any case are often based on false assumptions, and they were sincerely convinced that it would be preposterous to approve of the espousal of the values of a social structure that gives rise to unmerited suffering

---

2 By no means all the intertextual allusions have been considered in the previous chapters. For instance, the film *For Whom the Bell Tolls* (with Ingrid Bergman and Gary Cooper, dir. Sam Wood, 1943) (*RH* 239) echoes the *vie est ailleurs* syndrome that permeates the novel and is also a subtle indication of common human destiny. The latter theme is also suggested by the mention of Thomas Mann's *Las cabezas trocadas* (*The Transposed Heads*) (*BAA* 38), but this title's *raison d'être* may well have been the author's playful wish to signal his idiosyncratic technique of transposing dialogue, found in *El beso de la mujer araña* and in *Maldición eterna a quien lea estas páginas*. There are also slightly less obvious allusions, some of which may be judged equally ludic. One example is when Gladys notes that an embracing couple constitutes "una sola sombra" [a single shadow], a phrase from the Romantic poem "Nocturno" by the Colombian poet José Asunción Silva, who committed suicide in 1896. Furthermore, as Stephanie Merrim notes ("For a New [Psychological] Novel," 152), there is a reflection of the title (though not of the poems themselves) of Charles Baudelaire's *Les Fleurs du mal* (1857) in *Pubis angelical* (*Pa* 134).

3 They also reveal the absurdity of Angela Dellepiane's claim that Puig had no literary education. "Diez años de novela argentina," *Problemas de literatura* 1.1 (1972): 57–74 (71).

as a means of individual survival. Pathetic characters like Choli (*RH*), who is dedicated to superficial glamor in a quest for what cannot be achieved, and Molina, whose totally impossible dream is to become the wife of a traditionally heterosexual man, illustrated their thesis. The background to all this, they pointed out, was the pernicious patriarchy that, among other things, imbued women with a belief in the possibility of ineffable happiness provided they accepted their femininity, the only alternative being male disapproval and the withdrawal of love.[4]

It seems that none of this can be denied. There is no shortage of indications in the novels that this was indeed what the author thought, and he gave several interviews in which he condemned both social and political injustice. The problem, as I see it, is that careful reading of both his fiction and his interviews suggests that his feelings were at odds with his commonsense views.[5] It is debatable that his work constitutes an attack on the mass media, especially as the references are by no means limited to this area of culture. Even in the novels where it does predominate, it is hard to locate authorial condemnation: his love for the *géneros menores*, which are afforded detailed and affectionate attention, is similar to Cervantes's fascination for the chivalric novel, which is explicitly but unconvincingly criticized in *Don Quijote*.[6] He found the tensions of traditional male–female relationships seductive and, perhaps most important of all, there is never a hint of scorn in the novels toward any of his characters.

As has become clear, my contention is that the key to any reading of Puig is an awareness of fundamental authorial ambivalence vis-à-vis

---

4 See Eva Figes, *Patriarchal Attitudes* (1970; London: Macmillan, 1986) 26.

5 Philip Swanson ("Sailing Away on a Boat to Nowhere") takes this view even further:

> Puig's novels point simultaneously in all sorts of opposing and self-thwarting directions. This may be taken by some as an indication of the characteristic ambiguity of the Latin American "new novel" whose genesis is intimately connected with a loss of faith in the supposedly simple, black-and-white perceptions of reality that underlay the fiction of so-called traditional realism.

Although I link the term "new novel" to the Boom period and see Puig's works as part of what is now referred to as the *novísima narrativa* of the Post-Boom, I agree with Swanson.

6 See my article "Chivalry and 'Camp' Sensibility in *Don Quijote*, with Some Thoughts on the Novels of Manuel Puig," *Forum for Modern Language Studies* 26.2 (1990): 127–43, for more on the connection between Cervantes and Puig.

the question of change. (This emerged even in the interviews, some of which have been cited in the course of this study.) On a narrative level, there are few clues to help the reader draw straightforward conclusions—that there should be two schools of critical thought regarding the alleged happy endings is evidence of this—and it is surely no accident that the *impasse* is the most frequently found narrative device. This serves to highlight the frustration and pain that attend the countless vital choices that human beings are obliged to make. Reason may tell us that at least some of these could be eliminated, or made more tolerable, if social structures and personal attitudes were modified. Even problems that are constitutionally based, such as those stemming from the oedipal situation, may be exacerbated by the patriarchal superstructure. After all, as Malinowski pointed out, there are tribes that simply do not recognize the father-figure and are therefore immune to certain traumas.[7] Again, it is incontrovertible that Puig accepted this view. The determinism in his texts is not so blinkered and unaccommodating as to deny that difficult relationships between lovers, or between children and parents, could be improved if society were gentler, less exigent, and more flexible. However, there is no avoiding the ultimately fatalistic, even pessimistic, aspect of his determinism. Those rational, demythifying characters who do attempt to create a new world are neither happy nor particularly appealing, and the author's sympathy for those who are reluctant to relinquish the comfort and (perceived) advantages of faith in the old myths as represented in fiction is so patent as to suggest that his head and his heart were indeed at odds.

The reader is faced with the same kind of difficult choice as Puig's fictional creations: whether to approve of well-meaning characters with foolish ideas or unsympathetic people with eminently sensible ideas. This particular choice can be seen as artificially created and simplistic, and its morphology judged a product of a social system that is being challenged: it may be based on a myth as counterfeit as the stereotypes of the superior man or of the beautiful, virtuous woman. Most important of all, it may be claimed that if this myth ever was applicable, and therapeutic, it was relevant only for certain people in particular historical and geographical contexts. I suggest that this is precisely where the strength of all Puig's output lies: his was a contemporary vision of the traditional human hierarchy, of the values of the past,

---

7 Referred to by Figes, *Patriarchal Attitudes*, 14.

their legacy, and their current worth. In spite of his awareness of the existence of rational alternatives, it is my view that he could never quite bring himself to repudiate dedication to the sort of fatuous and life-threatening illusions that are now far less frequently found and that are best illustrated by the "hyperfeminine" Molina, one of the truly great creations in modern fiction. Puig had so much sympathy for those who embark on a quest for beauty and happiness in an ultimately doomed attempt to make "l'univers moins hideux et les instants moins lourds" [the universe less ugly and time less heavy][8] that he could not unequivocally adopt a demythifying approach, the result of which—as he saw it—is expressed by one of his creations who has tried in vain to find fulfilment through reason: "Viviremos sin tener que ser felices" [We'll survive without needing to be happy].[9]

---

8 Baudelaire, "Hymne à la beauté," from *Les Fleurs du mal.*

9 These words are spoken by Larry (*Me* 154).

Works Cited

BOOKS ON MANUEL PUIG

Bacarisse, Pamela. *The Necessary Dream: A Study of the Novels of Manuel Puig.* Cardiff: U of Wales P; Totowa, NJ: Barnes & Noble, 1988.

Campos, René Alberto. *Espejos: la textura cinemática en* La traición de Rita Hayworth. Madrid: Editorial Pliegos, 1985.

Echavarren, Roberto and Enrique Giordano. *Manuel Puig: Montaje y alteridad del sujeto.* Santiago, Chile: Instituto Profesional del Pacífico, 1986.

Ezquerro, Milagros. *Que raconter c'est apprendre à mourir: Essai d'analyse de "El beso de la mujer araña" de Manuel Puig.* Toulouse: U of Toulouse-Le Mirail: Institut d'Études Hispaniques et Hispano-Américaines, 1981.

García Ramos, Juan Manuel. *La narrativa de Manuel Puig. (Por una crítica en libertad).* La Laguna: U de La Laguna, 1981.

———, ed. *Manuel Puig.* Madrid: Ediciones de Cultura Hispánica, 1991.

Kerr, Lucille. *Suspended Fictions: Reading Novels by Manuel Puig.* Urbana: U of Illinois P, 1987.

Muñoz, Elías Miguel. *El discurso utópico de la sexualidad en Manuel Puig.* Madrid: Editorial Pliegos, 1987.

ARTICLES AND CHAPTERS ON PUIG

Alter, Robert. "Mimesis and the Motive for Fiction." *Tri-Quarterly* 42 (1978): 228–49.

Bacarisse, Pamela. "The Projection of Peronism in the Novels of Manuel Puig." *The Historical Novel in Latin America: A Symposium.* Ed. Daniel Balderston. Gaithersburg: Ediciones Hispamérica and Roger Thayer Stone Center for Latin American Studies, Tulane U, 1986. 185–99.

———. "Superior Men and Inferior Reality: Manuel Puig's *Pubis angelical.*" *Bulletin of Hispanic Studies* 66.1 (1989): 361–70.

———. "*Boquitas pintadas.*" *Landmarks in Contemporary Latin American Fiction.* Ed. Philip Swanson. London: Routledge, 1990: 207–21.

———. "Chivalry and 'Camp' Sensibility in *Don Quijote*, with Some Thoughts on the Novels of Manuel Puig." *Forum for Modern Language Studies* 26.2 (1990): 127–43.

———. "*Sangre de amor correspondido* de Manuel Puig: subjetividad, identidad y paranoia." *Revista Iberoamericana* 155–56 (1991): 469–79.

———. "Manuel Puig's *sentimiento trágico de la vida.*" *World Literature Today* 65.4 (1991): 631–36.

———. "Manuel Puig and the Uses of Culture." *The Review of Contemporary Fiction* 11.3 (1991): 197–207.

Borinsky, Alicia. "Castración y lujos." *Revista Iberoamericana* 90 (1975): 29–45.

———. *Ver/Ser visto (Notas para una analítica poética).* Barcelona: Antoni Bosch, 1978.

Christian, Karen S. "El mito del 'hombre superior' y la liberación de la mujer colonizada en *Pubis angelical.*" *Alba de América* 4.6–7 (1986): 93–103.

Dellepiane, Angela. "Diez años de novela argentina." *Problemas de literatura* 1.1 (1972): 7–72.

Gimferrer, Pere. *Radicalidades.* Barcelona: Antoni Bosch, 1978.

Goytisolo, Juan. "Manuel Puig: una novela política." *El viejo topo* (Supplement "Libros," December 1979).

Le Bigot, Claude. "Fantasme, mythe et parole dans *El beso de la mujer araña* de Manuel Puig." *Les Langues Néo-Latines* 75.3 (1981): 25–56.

Linenberg-Fressard, Raquel. "Les noms de personnage dans *La traición de Rita Hayworth*, de Manuel Puig." *Les Langues Néo-Latines* 3.254 (1985): 81–93.

———. "La motivation des noms de personnage dans *Pubis angelical* de Manuel Puig." *Imprévue* 1 (1986): 99–109.

Ludmer, Iris Josefina. "*Boquitas pintadas*: siete recorridos." *Actual* 2.8–9 (1971): 3–22.

MacAdam, Alfred J. *Modern Latin American Narratives: The Dreams of Reason.* Chicago: U of Chicago P, 1977. 91–101.

Macchi, Yves. "Fonction narrative des notes infrapaginales dans *El beso de La mujer araña* de Manuel Puig." *Les Langues Néo-Latines* 76 (1982): 67–81.

Magnarelli, Sharon. *The Lost Rib: Female Characters in the Spanish-American Novel*. Lewisburg, PA: Bucknell UP, 1985.

Merrim, Stephanie. "For a New (Psychological) Novel in the Works of Manuel Puig." *Novel: A Forum on Fiction* 17.2 (1984): 141–57.

Minard, Evelyne. "*La traición de Rita Hayworth*: violence et mort dans l'Argentine de Manuel Puig." *Cahiers du Monde Hispanique et Luso-Brésilien* 39 (1982): 75–80.

Molho, Maurice. "Tango de la madre araña." *Actes du Colloque sur l'Oeuvre de Puig et Vargas Llosa: Avril 1982*. Fontenay aux Roses: Les Cahiers de Fontenay, 1982. 161–68.

Morello-Frosch, Marta. "*La traición de Rita Hayworth*, o el nuevo arte de narrar películas." *Sin nombre* 4.1 (1970): 77–82.

———. "La sexualidad opresiva en las obras de Manuel Puig." *Nueva Narrativa Hispanoamericana* 5 (1975): 151–58.

Piglia, Ricardo. "Clase media: cuerpo y destino (una lectura de *La traición de Rita Hayworth* de Manuel Puig)." *Nueva Novela Latinoamericana*. Ed. J. Lafforgue. Vol. 2. Buenos Aires: Editorial Paidós, 1972. 2 vols. 350–62.

Rodríguez Monegal, Emir. "*La traición de Rita Hayworth*: una tarea de desmitificación." *Narradores de esta América*. Vol. 2. Buenos Aires: Editorial Alfa Argentina, 1974. 2 vols. 356–80.

———. "Los sueños de Evita: a propósito de la última novela de Manuel Puig." *Narradores de esta América*. Vol. 2. Buenos Aires: Editorial Alfa Argentina, 1974. 2 vols. 381–93.

Safir, Margery A. "Mitología: otro nivel de metalenguaje en *Boquitas pintadas*." *Revista Iberoamericana* 90 (1975): 47–58.

Sarduy, Severo. "Notas a las notas a las notas . . . a propósito de Manuel Puig." *Revista Iberoamericana* 37 (1971): 555–67.

Swanson, Philip. "Sailing Away on a Boat to Nowhere: *El beso de la mujer araña* and *Kiss of the Spider Woman*, from Novel to Film." *Essays on Hispanic Themes in Honour of Edward C. Riley*. Eds. Jennifer Lowe and Philip Swanson. Edinburgh: Dept. of Hispanic Studies, U of Edinburgh, 1989. 331–59.

Triviños, Gilberto. "La destrucción del verosímil folletinesco en *Boquitas pintadas*." *Texto Crítico* 9 (1976): 117–30.

Vich-Campos, Maryse. "L'invention de Molina (à propos du film *Cat People* dans *El beso de la mujer araña*, de Manuel Puig)." *Actes du Colloque sur l'Oeuvre de Puig et Vargas Llosa: Avril 1982*. Fontenay aux Roses: Les Cahiers de Fontenay, 1982. 107–13.

Yúdice, George. "*El beso de la mujer araña* y *Pubis angelical*: entre el placer y el saber." *Literature and Popular Culture*. Ed. Rose S. Minc. Gaithersburg: Ediciones Hispamérica and Montclair State College, 1981. 43–57.

INTERVIEWS WITH MANUEL PUIG

Fossey, Jean-Michel. *Galaxia Latinoamericana*. Las Palmas: Inventarios Provisionales, 1973. 137–52. (Interview)

Osorio, Manuel. "Entrevista con Manuel Puig." *Cuadernos para el diálogo* 231 (1977): 51–53. (Interview)

Pérez Luna, Elisabeth. "Con Manuel Puig en Nueva York." *Hombre del mundo* 8 (1978): 69–107. (Interview)

Quiblier, J.-Michel and J.-Pierre Joecker. "Entretien avec Manuel Puig." *Masques: Revue des homosexualités* 11 (1981): 29–32. (Interview)

Rodríguez Monegal, Emir. "El folletín rescatado." *Revista de la Universidad de México* 27.2 (1972): 27–35. (Interview)

Sosnowski, Saúl. "Manuel Puig: Entrevista." *Hispamérica* 3 (1973): 73. (Interview)

GENERAL

Allen, Rupert C. *Psyche and Symbol in the Theater of Federico García Lorca*. Austin: U of Texas P, 1974.

Allende, Isabel. *La casa de los espíritus*. Barcelona: Plaza y Janés, 1982.

Barbault, André. *Del psicoanálisis a la astrología*. Trans. Martha I. Moia. Buenos Aires: Editorial Dédalo, 1975. (Trans. of *De la Psychanalyse à l'astrologie*, 1961.)

Barthes, Roland. "L'Effet du réel." *Communications* 2 (1968): 84–89.

Baudrillard, Jean. *L'Échange symbolique et la mort*. Paris: Gallimard, 1976.

Beauvoir, Simone de. *The Second Sex*. Trans. H.M. Parshley. 1949; Harmondsworth: Penguin, 1972.

Berthelot, Marcellin. *Les Origines d'alchimie*. Paris, 1885.

Blanksten, George. *Perón's Argentina*. Chicago: U of Chicago P, 1953.

Breuer, Josef and Sigmund Freud. "Studies on Hysteria" (1895), *Standard Edition of the Complete Psychological Works of Sigmund Freud*. Trans. and ed. James Strachey, in collaboration with Anna Freud, 24 vols. London: Hogarth and Institute of Psycho-analysis, II.

Campbell, Joseph. *The Hero with a Thousand Faces*. 2nd ed. Princeton: Princeton UP, 1968.

Cazamian, L. *A History of French Literature*. 1955; Oxford: Oxford UP, 1960.

Chasseguet-Smirgel, Janine and Béla Grunberger. *Freud or Reich? Psychoanalysis and Illusion*. Trans. Claire Pajaczkowska. New Haven: Yale UP, 1986.

Chatman, Seymour. *Coming to Terms: The Rhetoric of Narrative in Fiction and Film*. Ithaca: Cornell UP, 1990.

Chevalier, Jean and Alain Gheerbrant. *Dictionnaire des Symboles*. Paris: Robert Laffont and Éditions Jupiter, 1982.

Cirlot, Juan-Eduardo. *Diccionario de símbolos*. Barcelona: Editorial Labor, 1969.

Comas, Juan. *Racial Myths*. Paris: UNESCO, 1951.

Cordova, Richard de. "The Emergence of the Star System and the Bourgeoisifi-cation of the American Cinema." *Star Signs*. London: British Film Institute, 1982.

Daiches, David. *A Critical History of English Literature*. 2 vols. London: Secker & Warburg, 1960.

Debicki, Andrew. *Antología de la poesía mexicana moderna*. London: Tamesis, 1977.

Dijkstra, Bram. *Idols of Perversity: Fantasies of Feminine Evil in Fin-de-Siècle Culture*. New York: Oxford UP, 1986.

Edwards, Jonathan. *Sinners in the Hands of an Angry God*. Boston, 1742.

Eliade, Mircea. *Myths, Dreams and Mysteries*. Trans. Philip Mairet. London: Collins, 1972. (Trans. of *Mythes, Rêves et mystères*, 1957.)

Engels, F. "Letter to Franz Mehring, 14 July 1893." Karl Marx and Friedrich Engels. *Basic Writings on Politics and Philosophy*. Ed. L. Feuer. London: Fontana, 1969.

Fest, Joachim C. *Hitler*. Trans. Richard and Clara Winston. 1973; Harmonds-worth: Penguin, 1977.

Fiedler, Leslie. *What Was Literature? Class Culture and Mass Society*. 1982; New York: Simon, 1984.

Figes, Eva. *Patriarchal Attitudes*. 1970; London: Macmillan, 1986.

Forgacs, David. "Marxist Literary Theories." *Modern Literary Theory: A Comparative Introduction*. Eds. Ann Jefferson and David Robey. 2nd ed. London: B.T. Batsford, 1986. 166–203.

Foucault, Michel. *Histoire de la Sexualité: La Volonté de savoir*. Paris: Gallimard, 1976.

Franco, Jean. *An Introduction to Spanish-American Literature*. Cambridge: Cambridge UP, 1969.

———. *A Literary History of Spain: Spanish American Literature since Indepen-dence*. London: Ernest Benn, 1973.

Freud, Sigmund. *Standard Edition of the Complete Psychological Works*. 24 vols. Trans. and ed. James Strachey, in collaboration with Anna Freud. London: Hogarth and Institute of Psycho-analysis, 1953–74.

Fromm, Erich. *The Fear of Freedom*. 1942; London: Routledge, 1960.

———. *Man for Himself: An Enquiry into the Psychology of Ethics*. 1947; New York: Fawcett, 1969.

———. *Greatness and Limitations of Freud's Thought*. London: Jonathan Cape, 1980.

Fry, Peter and Edward MacRae. *O que é a Homossexualidade*. São Paulo: Editora Brasiliense, 1983.

Frye, Northrop. *The Great Code: The Bible and Literature*. 1981; London: Routledge, 1983.

Gauquelin, Michel. *Astrology and Science*. Trans. James Hughes. London: Granada, 1972. (Trans. of *L'Astrologie devant la science*, 1966.)

González Tuñón, Raúl. *A la sombra de los barrios amados*. Buenos Aires: Editorial Lautaro, 1957.

Goodheart, Eugene. *Desire and its Discontents*. New York: Columbia UP, 1991.

Graham-Youll, Andrew. "Manuel Puig." *The Independent* (London, 24 July 1990): 12.

Graves, Robert. *The White Goddess: A Historical Grammar of Poetic Myth*. London: Faber, 1961.

Haftmann, Werner. *Painting in the Twentieth Century*. 2 vols. 1961; London: Lund Humphries, 1965.

Halliwell, Leslie. *Halliwell's Film Guide*. 2nd ed. London: Granada, 1982.

Haralovich, Mary Beth. "Woman's Proper Place: Defining Gender Roles in Film and History." Unpublished paper for an independent study with Professor Jeanne Allen, U of Wisconsin–Madison, 1979.

Haskell, Molly. *From Reverence to Rape: The Treatment of Women in the Movies*. Harmondsworth: Penguin, 1979.

Hatfield, Henry. *Modern German Literature: The Major Figures in Context*. London: Edward Arnold, 1966.

Hillman, James. *Emotion: A Comprehensive Phenomenology of Theories and their Meanings for Therapy*. London: Routledge, 1960.

Honorius of Autun. "Speculum de mysteriis ecclesiae." *Patrologiae cursus completus*. Ed. Jacques Paul Migne. 221 vols. Latin Series 172, cols. 807–1108. Paris, 1844–64.

Hume, David. *Of the Standard of Taste, and Other Essays*. Indianapolis: Bobbs Merrill, 1965.

Huxley, Aldous. *Ends and Means: An Enquiry into the Nature of Ideals and into the Methods Employed for their Realization*. London: Chatto & Windus, 1938.

Huyssen, Andreas. *After the Great Divide: Modernism, Mass Culture and Postmodernism*. Bloomington: Indiana UP; London: Macmillan, 1986.

Janeway, Elizabeth. *Man's World, Woman's Place*. New York: Dell, 1971.

Jung, C.G. *Modern Man in Search of a Soul*. 1953; London: Routledge, 1962.

———. *Memories, Dreams, Reflections*. Rec. and ed. Anniela Jaffé. Trans. Richard and Clara Winston. London: Fontana, 1983. (Trans. of *Errinerungen, Träume, Gedenken*, 1961.)

———. *Alchemical Studies*. Trans. R.F.C. Hull. New York: Bollingen Foundation, 1967.

Keppler, C.F. *The Literature of the Second Self*. Tucson: U of Arizona P, 1972.

Kohlberg, L. "A Cognitive–Developmental Analysis of Children's Sex-Role Concepts and Attitudes." *The Development of Sex Differences*. Ed. E.E. Maccoby. Stanford: Stanford UP, 1966.

Kristeva, Julia. *Strangers to Ourselves*. Trans. Leon S. Roudiez. New York: Columbia UP, 1991. (Trans. of *Étrangers à nous-mêmes*, 1988.)

Kuhn, Annette. *Women's Pictures: Feminism and Cinema*. London: Routledge, 1982.

Lacan, Jacques. *Écrits*. Trans. Alan Sheridan. London: Tavistock, 1948.

Laing, R.D. *The Politics of Experience.* Harmondsworth: Penguin, 1967.

Lamarr, Hedy. *Ecstasy and Me: My Life as a Woman.* London: W.H. Allen, 1967.

Laplace, Maria. "Producing and Consuming the Woman's Film." *Home is Where the Heart Is: Studies in Melodrama and the Woman's Film.* Ed. Christine Gledhill. London: British Film Institute, 1987: 138–66.

McConnell, Frank D. *The Spoken Seen: Film and the Romantic Imagination.* Baltimore: Johns Hopkins UP, 1975.

MacQuarrie, John. *Existentialism.* 1972; Harmondsworth: Penguin, 1976.

Mitchell, Juliet. *Psychoanalysis and Feminism.* 1974; Harmondsworth: Penguin, 1982.

Mitchell, Juliet and Jacqueline Rose, eds. *Feminine Sexuality: Jacques Lacan and the École Freudienne.* Trans. Jacqueline Rose. London: Macmillan, 1982.

Moi, Toril. *Sexual/Textual Politics.* London: Methuen, 1985.

Morales y Marín, José Luis. *Diccionario de iconología y simbología.* Madrid: Taurus, 1984.

Nervo, Amado. *Poemas* (1901).

Neumann, Erich. *The Great Mother: An Analysis of the Archetype.* Trans. Ralph Manheim. 2nd ed. Princeton: Princeton UP, 1963.

———. *The Origins and History of Consciousness.* Trans. R.F.C. Hull. 1954; London: Routledge, 1973.

Ortiz, Mecha. *Mecha Ortiz.* Buenos Aires: Editorial Moreno, 1982.

Pater, Walter. *The Renaissance: Studies in Art and Poetry.* 1873; London: Collins, 1961.

Phillips, Rachel. *Alfonsina Storni: From Poetess to Poet.* London: Tamesis, 1975.

Pogrebin, Letty Cottin. "Competing with Women." *Ms* 1.2 (1972): 78.

Prince, Gerald. *A Dictionary of Narratology.* Lincoln: U of Nebraska P, 1987.

Rank, Otto. *Truth and Reality.* Trans. Jessie Taft. 1936; New York: Norton, 1978.

Reik, Theodor. *The Creation of Woman.* New York: McGraw-Hill, 1960.

Rose, H.J. *A Handbook of Greek Mythology.* 1928; London: Methuen, 1964.

Rougemont, Denis de. *Passion and Society.* Trans. Montgomery Belgion. London: Faber, 1962.

Sábato, Ernesto. *El otro rostro del peronismo: Carta abierta a Mario Amadeo.* Buenos Aires: Imprenta López, 1956.

Sánchez, Luis Rafael. "Apuntación mínima de lo soez." *Literature and Popular Culture in the Hispanic World.* Ed. Rose S. Minc. Gaithersburg: Ediciones Hispamérica and Montclair State College, 1981. 9–14.

Saunier, Marc. *La Légende des symboles.* Paris: E. Sansot, 1911.

Silberer, Herbert. *Hidden Symbolism of Alchemy and the Occult Arts.* Trans. Smith Ely Jelliffe. New York: Dover, 1971. (Formerly entitled *Problems of Mysticism and its Symbolism*: New York: Moffat, Yard & Co., 1917.)

Spender, Dale. *Man Made Language.* 2nd ed. London: Routledge, 1985.

Szichman, Mario. *A las 20:25, la señora entró en la inmortalidad.* Hanover, NH: Ediciones del Norte, 1980.

Thomson, David. *A Biographical Dictionary of the Cinema*. London: Secker & Warburg, 1975.

Tibón, Gutierre. *Diccionario de nombres propios*. 2nd ed. Mexico City: Fondo de Cultura Económica, 1986.

Todorov, Tsvetan. *Mikhail Bakhtin: The Dialogic Principle*. Trans. Wlad Godzich. Manchester: Manchester UP, 1984.

Ulla, Noemí. *Tango, rebelión y nostalgia*. Buenos Aires: Editorial Jorge Alvarez, 1967.

Updike, John. "Nobody Gets Away with Everything." *The New Yorker* 25 May 1992: 84–88.

Urgosikova, B. "*Kanal*." *The International Dictionary of Films and Filmmakers*. Ed. Christopher Lyon. Vol. 1. London: Firethorn, 1986. 236. 2 vols.

Warner, Marina. *Alone of All her Sex: The Myth and Cult of the Virgin Mary*. London: Weidenfeld & Nicolson, 1976.

Weeks, Jeffrey. *Sexuality and its Discontents: Meanings, Myths and Modern Sexualities*. London: Routledge, 1985.

Westwater, Angela K. "Action Painting." *The Fontana Dictionary of Modern Thought*. Eds. Alan Bullock and Oliver Stallybrass. London: Fontana–Collins, 1977.

Woll, Allen L. *The Latin American Image in American Film*. Los Angeles: UCLA Latin Amer. Center Publ., 1977.

Index of References

General Index